IT'S ALL RELATIVE… THE GOD FACTOR…

How I view our universe

Mr. Anthony L. Calistro Jr.

"God does not play dice with the universe" – Albert Einstein

Copyright © 2013 Mr. Anthony L. Calistro Jr.
All rights reserved.
ISBN: 0615821189
ISBN 13: 9780615821184
Library of Congress Control Number: 2013941010
It's All Relative...The God Factor, Burnsville, MN
U.S. Library of Congress & U.S. Copyright Office
1-929291781
05/01/2013

TABLE OF CONTENTS

Introduction Who I am and what this book is about 1
My Faith and My Experiences with Faith 9
The Shroud of Turin 15
My Theory 21
Dimensions 23
The Brain 27
Einstein's Theory of Relativity 29
Near-Death and Out-of-Body Experiences 41
My Theory (Part B)Is God A Universal Brain? 53
String Theory 65
Superstring Theory 67
The Particle Accelerator 71
Nature and the Language of Opposites 81
Black Holes and White Holes 85
Matter and Antimatter 89
Dark Matter and Dark Energy 93
Mother Earth or Mother Universe 99
Life and Death 103
How Science and Religion Compare 109
The Alpha and the Omega 113
ConclusionWhat I Think Einstein Was Truly After 115

ACKNOWLEDGMENTS

First and foremost, I want to dedicate this book to God for opening my eyes. I personally feel that I know my place in the universe, and God showed me that no matter where I end up in this universe, he will be with me. So I want to say thank you for always being there and for blessing me. I know you have not forgotten me, because, on a daily basis, you provide everything I need. No matter how dark things seem, I have always had food, protection, and shelter. By keeping me humble and giving me hard times, you have shown me how truly rich I am. If I lost my possessions in a fire tomorrow, I know that I would survive without them. I know the only thing that would keep me alive if I were to lose my family in a fire tomorrow is God. By opening my eyes, I see just how rich and blessed I truly am. Thank you for your continued blessings and promises and for saving my soul. Amen.

Second, I want to thank my daughter, Brooke. You are my whole world, and I love you more every day. You are the sum of my possessions in this world. Your little smiles and "I love you, Daddy," keep going when I think I have nothing left. Then I remember what God gave me, and I have the strength to keep going. You make me want to be the best I can be. Thank you and I will love you forever.

Third, I want to thank my wife, Tiffani. You gave me my whole world! I know we have had our ups and downs, but we are still together. I think the universe wanted us to be together, because you gave me the child I know I was meant to have. Thank you for being my opposite in this crazy universe and for making my world whole. I love you. Thank you for sticking by me while I wrote this book. I especially thank you for enduring all those nights I spent absorbed in my own universe, thinking and then writing this book to get my thoughts out. Thank you for being my first and best critic and for not thinking I was going crazy even when I thought I was at times. Thank you for just believing in me, sticking beside me, and just generally picking up the extra slack while I was doing this. Thank you for being my other half, my opposite.

Finally, I want to dedicate this book to humanity everywhere. In my view, if only one person opens his or her mind to God as a result of reading this book, then I will have been successful. I was meant to write this book, so someone must be meant to read it. Every action has an equal and opposite reaction in this universe. Also, this is my own personal test of faith. When people read this book, they are either going to see the points I am trying to make and understand the connections for themselves or they aren't going to understand and will tear my viewpoint to shreds. In this book, I discuss my faith and religion and how science can help us to search for God.

I believe humanity needs to come together *as a species* to figure out this universe. I'm no better than anyone else out there, and I know I'm special in God's eyes. That means you are, too! Everyone is! So we seriously need to start thinking about why we are here before we destroy each other in war! That's why this book is dedicated to everyone else out there: *Everyone.*

Religion tells me who created the universe; science tells me how it was done. - Unknown.

I also want to give a special thanks to my parents. I thank my mom for giving me that extra push to actually write this book instead of just thinking about writing it, and I want to thank my dad for *always* pushing me to be better and for never letting me be satisfied with an average life. Thank you for always pushing me.

Anthony Lee Calistro Jr.

INTRODUCTION
Who I am and what this book is about

If you were to walk into a mall and ask fifty people what they thought was out in our universe, how many different answers would you get? I ask myself this question all the time, and I wonder if other people have ever possibly had the same thoughts I do. Could God be out there along with alien life? Why does it have to be only other life-forms? Why can't it also be God? I think we really can find God; and I think there is strong scientific evidence to suggest that God could be out there. If we opened our minds up and used science to see what's around us, then we might discover a whole new world in front of our very eyes! I like to take the scientific evidence and theories and then look at them from a different angle. I call it the God factor. So, if I were one of those fifty people you asked about the universe, then this book would be my answer. It's how I imagine our universe—from how I look at life and what I think is out there to how I visually imagine the universe after all the theories and scientific facts I have heard. Once I know the scientific theories, I look at it from my angle, and because I am religious, I add the God factor.

First, I want to tell you a little bit about myself—about my faith and why I believe in God. I have had a few experiences that have shown me that God is with me. I am what you would call average. I go to work every day like everybody else; I'm no astrophysicist, quantum physicist, I actually studied architecture. I love things that have both a technical and artistic aspect. Leonardo da Vinci was one of my heroes because he also would see the universe and life with both a scientific and artistic aspects. I am just like you, but I like to think about the universe a lot. I feel I am nothing special, except to God. I can't run marathons, calculate advanced math, or sing a beautiful song. But I am unique, and I can think big. One of God's blessings is my ability to think for myself. I form my own opinions based on the evidence. Keep that in mind when you hear the evidence and my theory: form your own opinion, and think for yourself!

I have always been intrigued by the science vs. God debate. Deep in my heart, I know God is eventually going to win. Now the science vs. God debate basically boils down to three simple questions about life. The first is: where did we come from and how did we get here (both physically and spiritually)? The second is: why are we here? The third is: where do we go when we die? Modern science still can't answer these questions for me; it can't answer any questions about the soul. All science says is that we don't know where we came from spiritually or that we don't have souls. Scientists will tell us that we grew from cells. They will say we evolved from other animals. To me, that is not enough to conclusively disprove God's role in our creation or the creation of the universe. That just sounds like bad science in my opinion. Every reaction has an equal and opposite reaction in this universe. If I have a physical body, then I must have a spiritual one. Until you can prove I don't have a soul, why leave God out of science? Aren't we trying to figure out the meaning of life? Evolution is simply the process of life changing from one form to another.

Prove to me souls don't exist. If God is our "universal entity," an entity is something that is everywhere. Time cannot affect something that is everywhere. Time is not a factor for God! So, if God is an entity and everywhere, then he is zero dimensional. If time is not a factor for God, why couldn't he be responsible for our evolution? To me, it would sure be a bad design if humans couldn't evolve. Or perhaps God just knew what he was doing by creating evolution and allowing us to grow and learn. If time is no factor to God, then human creation, even at the cellular level, seems possible! Since time does not exist for God, who is our "universal entity," he has an eternity to create life! If science refutes God, where is the evidence for doing so? Prove to me you know where my spirit goes when I die. I know where my body goes, but, where does that part of me go that loves my daughter? Where does that part of me go that hurts when she hurts? I know that part of me is real. When science can prove to me that my soul does not exist, then I will believe science has disproved God's existence.

Introduction Who I am and what this book is about

Yet, God and religion can reveal to me the answers to life's questions. Where did I come from? I came from God. I am his child, made in his image. What's the meaning of life, and why are we here? Simple: we are here to love each other and treat each other as we want to be treated. It's a pretty simple universal law that people seem to know, even if they don't follow it. Second, when you figure that life is about love and not hate, teach other people to do the same. Where do I go when I die? I either go to heaven or I go to hell. That's it: simple. If God, our "universal entity," is everywhere and time is not a factor, how can time even exist if you're everywhere? The idea of souls spending eternity in heaven and hell certainly seems like a real possibility to me. If the risk of going to either heaven or hell could be real, I am certainly going to rethink my actions in life! If I know I have a soul, and I believe there could be some "universal entity" out there, and time is no factor for an entity, then heaven and hell could certainly be real! Religion answers all the questions very simply and it seems to be plain common sense.

Science calls God's miracles "chaos theory." These are occurrences that science and man can't explain. Scientists refer to these events as random events in nature or evolution. Religion calls them life, God's miracles, and God's plan. *Remember our "universal entity" is time, or should I say Father Time, and he controls it.* Life consists of the normal events that happen around us every day, then God creates new forms of life, and science calls this evolution. Religion refers to these new forms of life as nature's miracles or simply part of God's plan. God creating new forms of life and evolution of these animals are possible if time is not a factor.

Science compares miracles to violations of the laws of nature or physics, yet when they say this, they are comparing physics (our physical universe) to nature, something that is alive! To me, our universe is physical, biological, and spiritual. We live on this planet with lots of other life. Our universe is definitely alive, and the vast majority of us who do believe in God are not crazy! Therefore, I see three components to our universe when science seems to only study one. It's definitely possible that there are specimens in this universe that are undiscovered, including God!

Now, everyone reading this book needs to think, "What do I feel inside *myself*?" Do you feel something physical that you can see and touch? Or do you feel something natural and biological or spiritual? If you said something natural, then read this book to the end to see what I have to say! As you read, just keep remembering, you yourself said you feel something natural, not physical. If you said something physical, then I hope you read this book, maybe I can change your mind.

Science says miracles don't happen anymore or we would have evidence of their existence. Science says, show me a miracle and I will believe it. Miracles are everywhere if you open your eyes! Would you consider the birth of your child to be a miracle? How many people have ever prayed for someone who has had a critical injury or was severely ill? How many times have we heard doctors say someone won't recover only to be proved wrong? Go tell those people miracles don't exist.

What about the people who have had near-death experiences and believe that God saved them? Tell those people miracles are not real and that they don't exist. How about the soldier who prays to God to let him live one more day as he faces death? Go ask some of those people if miracles and God do not exist. Until you yourself have faced death personally, how can you call someone else crazy for believing in God? Go ask a parent who has prayed over a child they thought they were going to lose and didn't if miracles don't exist. Go ask doctors and surgeons if they believe in the existence of miracles. I bet a few would affirm that miracles exist! I bet we would find a lot more evidence of miracles around us if we just looked, opened our eyes, and believed they could exist! Your brain will see what you want it to see!

Science also says logic is determined by nature. My point exactly, but nature does not just consist of physical objects; nature is alive and biological! Nature is not just rocks and stars; it's also every living thing in between! That's why I think physics needs to include a biological aspect of life, because we are physical objects, but we are also biological objects, and if you're religious, we are also spiritual objects.

That's why I don't think physics alone will ever explain the whole universe. There is more to the universe than physics. If there is more to it than just physics, and the universe is physical/biological/spiritual,

INTRODUCTION Who I am and what this book is about

then I do not think only math will give us all the answers. We need a new universal language, a natural language. How about patterns in nature like positive and negative, black and white, light and day, big and small? Patterns can represent numbers universally because patterns stay the same. If we do actually encounter alternate life in space, who's to say that we would be able to communicate using visual numbers? Visual numbers are something humans created! How do you interpret math if you don't speak our language? I think what we are searching for in space is right here on earth, and it's talking to us. Nature is alive, so why couldn't it try to communicate with us?

Why does God have to be some supernatural thing we made up? Why can't he be something natural we just haven't discovered yet? Remember, God is an entity that is everywhere, so time is no factor for him. Since he is an entity, he is not physical; therefore he can't die! Only physical things can die. Why can't God be the whole universe that's alive, both the physical part that can die and the entity that is everywhere and eternal? Isn't God supposed to be everything; the Alpha and the Omega, the beginning and the end? People picture some giant man without a head sitting next to Jesus in heaven, but when you think about it, God is the universe! The physical and nonphysical, the action and the equal and opposite reaction!

I once watched a televised debate on science versus religion, and it was actually called "Science refutes God: the Debate."

In this debate four different scientists debated the issue, and it was two against two. During this debate, the religious side mentioned the big bang theory and how it was a miracle because it defied natural laws and created the universe. The scientists who were not religious responded that the creation of the universe was not a miracle; it was just a theory scientists used to explain the origin of the universe. Why can't it be both? Why can't it still be considered a miracle? The universe was created, set in motion, and life began, including human life. I would call that pretty miraculous! Why can't it still be a miracle that science can explain? I believe God created the miracle of the big bang, and science just finally figured out the process.

I'm not saying there is proof of God; I'm saying he definitely *could have* created our physical universe. Also during this debate, the philosophers made the point that scientists had not yet found proof of alien life but did not refute the possibility. Why is looking for God out in space crazier than looking for aliens out in space? Is this because we didn't see him the first time we went into space? Is that a reason to assume he is not there and push back thousands of years of instinct—the instinct that God has been with us since humans were first able to look at the stars and wonder where we came from. Why do we still believe aliens are out there even though humans have not yet encountered them? It's possible for both God and aliens to be out there. Yet in our society, you are normal for believing in aliens and crazy for believing in God. I do think aliens are out there, but I don't think we can see them with our level of vision. Yet we have hints of possible life out there. I believe we need to use our spirits to contact them, and I will get into that later in the book, as I explore my theory.

When I say "my theory," I mean my idea of how the universe could work. This is simply my opinion. The last part of the debate I want to bring up is this question a woman asked during the question/answer portion. She asked, "Neither side has described what God actually is or means to them." The Christians immediately said, "We thought we were clear. We are talking about Christianity and Jesus Christ." The scientists replied, "We imagine *a guiding universal entity that controls the universe.*" *To me, that is what God is; "a universal entity" controlling the universe.* I think universal brain could be the right idea, and it's a theory from astrophysicists.

Simply put, the "universal brain" controls the universe. That sure sounds like how I think of God, if I wanted to try to describe him scientifically! Again, I will get into more detail on this later in my theory. Now that I have brought up how science and religion have been battling it out, I'm going to describe just a couple personal experiences that illustrate God's presence in my life. I will then tell you my theory **and let you think for yourself about what you believe is out there.**

Since I do feel I need to write this book for people to read, I also want to know what the world thinks of this book! I want your opinion on my ideas. Maybe other people out there agree/semi-agree with me and will see their own universe more clearly. I want people to think when they read this and discuss their response to my ideas. That's the whole point of writing this book! I WANT to hear your opinions, to hear what you think.

I want to try to paint a picture in your mind. I know that trying to convey my thoughts to you will be hard, but I will try so you can get a view of my universe. I may repeat myself at different times, but it's only so you can follow my thought process along. I want to firmly plant each concept before jumping to my next thought. In this book, you will see I believe that God and nature are the missing factors in our physics-driven understanding of the universe. I am saying right here and now that I have never gone to school to study any of this stuff. I'm just like the other 99 percent of us who aren't astrophysicists or quantum physicists. I still wonder how I fit into this universe and where I came from.

This is not a book of scientific equations; it's a philosophy book filled with ideas of possibility. I try to look at the big picture and connect the dots of life. In this book I will look at dimensions, why I think the brain and life, and near-death and out-of-body experiences could all be key factors. I will tell you how I see Einstein's theory of relativity fitting in with the brain and "my theory." I talk about universal brain more in depth and how I believe that is scientifically God. I also discuss the possibility of physics and quantum physics working together to offer a richer explanation of the universe. I share my theory on black holes, white holes, wormholes, and more. So let's talk about my faith for just a minute, because my whole theory hinges on God and nature!

MY FAITH AND MY EXPERIENCES WITH FAITH

I want to start out by saying right here and now that I am a Christian. I have always been a Christian, and I always will be until the day I die. My faith began when I was little and went to church with my parents. I was saved and baptized around the age of four, and ever since then I have always felt a connection with God. I went to a Christian private school during pre-school and kindergarten, but from there I attended regular public schools. Between the ages of ten and twenty-five, I knew God was still with me, but I no longer practiced my faith.

My parents had divorced by then, and both quit going to church. I also quit going to church. I never did lose that connection with God, though, and I always felt a connection with nature and the universe. I also always felt that God and I were "good" on a different level. I believed, but I didn't practice what I believed. Then, a few experiences changed how I looked at everything! Those experiences told me that God was with me and had a plan for me, and that I needed to start truly believing. There have been many moments when I thought God was intervening in my life, but two experiences really stand out to me. They were both car accidents.

These car accidents are why I believe in God. These car accidents opened my eyes to the way I think, why I believe in God, and why I try to practice what I truly believe. They're why I realized God and I were not as "good" as I thought, even though I had been saved. I think God was pushing me to see the light even more clearly, and that's when I truly felt saved. Now I do feel like I know my place in the universe.

The first car accident happened when I was sixteen. My girlfriend's friend was driving us to my house. We were sitting at an intersection in town when the accident happened. My girlfriend's friend was driving, my girlfriend was the passenger, and I was in the backseat by myself, unbuckled.

We were trying to make a left turn, and we had to wait for oncoming traffic to pass us before we could turn. I was not really paying attention to what she was doing, since I was in the back, but I remember the car started to turn, and I heard my girlfriend scream. I looked up just in time to see a Volkswagen Beetle doing about forty miles per hour coming right at us. That was the last thing I really remember besides the crunching sound of the cars smashing together. We got hit directly on the passenger side as we turned, a perfect T-bone. A few friends from school happened to be in the car next to us at the intersection, and they later told me they had seen the whole thing.

One friend told me that when we got hit, he had seen me fly across the car, smash my head against the opposite door, and BOUNCE back up.

I remember coming to a few moments after the crash and realizing we had been hit. I didn't really know I was hurt at first. I remember feeling the bump with my hand and asking my girlfriend how bad it was. She said it was huge but not bleeding. The only people hurt in the crash were the other driver and me; the other driver had split his forehead open and was pretty bloody.

The ambulance and police came and checked everyone out and said the other driver needed stitches, and I needed to go to the hospital to be checked out. I did not want to go to the hospital, although I probably should have. I probably did have a mild concussion now that I think about it. I ended up with a lump on my head that didn't go away for a couple months and a bruise that covered almost my entire face for about two months. To this day, I can still feel the edge of that bump on my skull. In the end, I ended up OK. I was lucky!

From that point on, though, I was always paranoid about traveling in cars—whether riding or driving, it didn't matter. Deep inside I would always tense up while traveling in cars, and I was especially nervous about making left turns. After that car wreck, I developed a deep feeling I was going to die in a wreck someday. I had also known a couple different friends who were killed in separate car wrecks right after mine. Deep down, that paranoid feeling kept growing.

About ten years later, I had my second car wreck. By this point my fear of dying in another car accident had faded, but it was still always there a little bit. I was driving to work this time. I had just stopped and gotten coffee and gas at the gas station. This gas station was at another four-way stop light. When I pulled out of the gas station, I was immediately stuck at a red light.

I was sitting at the light behind three or four other cars when I looked up into my rearview mirror and saw a car coming at me way too fast! I had only the time it took me to make that observation before I got hit. Now, I was in a Ford Explorer with my brakes on at a dead stop, and a woman hit me with a Mazda 6 and pushed me about fifteen feet! Traffic travels on this road between forty-five and fifty miles per hour, and I took the impact. My lights went out again for the second time in my life.

This time I had my seat belt on, thank God. I had at least learned one lesson from the previous crash. As I said before, I was sitting behind a few other cars at that light. When I got hit, I did not smash into the cars ahead of me like one would expect but managed to end up on the median of the road, sitting beside the cars I had been behind.

Now, I have no idea how I had managed not to smash into the cars in front of me, and or how I landed on the median instead of being pushed into oncoming traffic. I managed to swerve around the cars in front of me. I know I usually stop a little closer to other cars than I should, so I would have had to really cut my wheel to miss those cars and then cut it back the other way in order to end up on the median. In my mind, there was no way I could have reacted fast enough to do all that during the impact of the crash.

She hit me hard enough that both vehicles were totaled out and both had to be sent on flat beds to the junk yard. The front end of her car was still attached to the back of my truck when our cars were towed away. Like I said, thank God I had buckled up that time, or I probably would have been really hurt.

That paranoid feeling of dying in a car accident was definitely back again, always there in the back of my mind. So life went on. I got a new car (one loaded with airbags), and I kept on going to work, driving by that same spot every day. Every time I passed that spot, I would ask myself how I could have missed the cars in front of me and still avoid oncoming traffic. For the longest time, I could only conclude that right before the impact, my subconscious mind and reflexes must have responded faster than I could think. In my head and heart, though, I knew that it had to have been God saving my butt. I just knew I didn't do it. I barely had time to notice the car that hit me. But, it was the only logical explanation.

Every time I drove by that spot, I would think about the accident and how I thought I might die in a wreck someday. Then I read a book, and no, it was not the Bible. So what could have changed the way I was feeling and thinking? What could I have read, aside from the Bible that would have changed my mind and how I felt about dying in car wrecks? It was a book about a six-year-old boy's car wreck, which should have been fatal. Instead, he lived and claimed he had been to heaven!

In *The Boy Who Came Back from Heaven* by Kevin and Alex Malarkey, a father and his child were driving home from church of all places. After stopping at a park, they headed home and were in a very bad car wreck. I highly recommend this book to anyone; it's a very inspirational story!

During this accident, the father was thrown from the car and ended up coming out of it fairly uninjured. His six-year-old son was a different story. He was severely injured, and at one point people on the scene had thought he was dead. He was still alive, however, and people who showed up at the scene prayed for him. When the air medic showed up in the helicopter and flew him to the hospital, that medic prayed for him. When they landed, the medic told his mom to pray for him, and from that point on, everyone who visited prayed. He was in a coma.

The father describes the child's injuries as an internal decapitation. That's all I'm going to say about his injuries; they were horrible. When I read the book as a dad, I felt the pain the father must have felt. The doctors did not expect the child to live, but the parents believed! The boy, Alex, ended up living, and I would call that a miracle! When Alex finally came out of his coma a few months later, he eventually ended up talking about his experiences in heaven with the angels. There was one part of his story that really stuck with me, and that's why I am sharing his story with you.

During their accident, the father was thrown from the car and sustained only minor injuries, and when his son started describing the accident and his near-death experience with heaven and angels, this is what he described. He said that he had seen angels "carry" his dad out of the car. That's when I wondered if angels had kept me from getting smashed between those cars during my last accident. I have to honestly say, I think that's how I managed to stay uninjured during my second accident. Deep down, I just knew it was not me; I knew I could not have physically reacted fast enough.

Ever since I had the idea that God or his angels must have protected me during those car accidents, my fear of dying in a car accident has gone away. Now I feel like I'm going to be around for a long time. I know it sounds crazy, but everyone has those deep-down thoughts and feelings—that was one of mine, and now it's gone! It's amazing how relieved a little faith can make you feel!

I have had too many little experiences, thoughts, and close calls with death to doubt that God is watching over me. These experiences have all led me to start following my faith, not just saying I believe it.

THE SHROUD OF TURIN

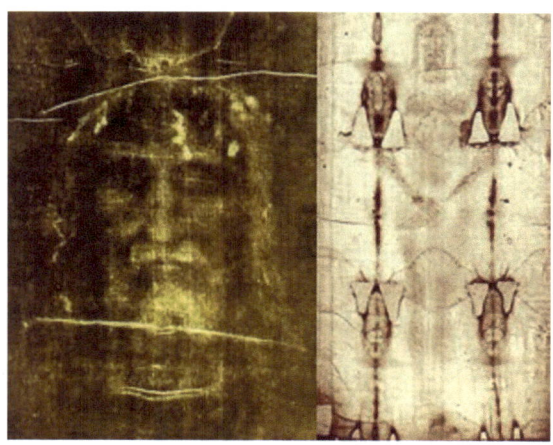

Is this the real face of Jesus Christ?
A photograph of "The Shroud of Turin"

The Shroud of Turin, for people who don't know, is the cloth that people believe was used to wrap Jesus's body after his crucifixion. This cloth is special not only because people believe it covered Jesus but also because there was an imprint of a total figure (face and body) upon the shroud. There have been a lot of different studies and experiments performed on the shroud to prove its authenticity. The History Channel recently aired a documentary on the shroud called *The Real Face of Jesus*.

This documentary was about the shroud's imprint, and scientists and graphic artists were going to try to re-create a 3D image of the face of Jesus. They were trying to create the most realistic looking model of Jesus the world has ever seen, and they did!

This show was interesting to me for several reasons. The first is pretty obvious, and that is the imprint left on the shroud. I have only seen the shroud on television, and when I saw it, as faded as it was, I knew I was looking at Jesus. Later in the show, they mention that no one has actually seen Jesus since he died two thousand years ago! Yet, the image of that imprint is exactly how everyone imagines Jesus!

It is funny how no one has seen him in two thousand years, and yet all the images we create of him all look so similar. Don't you think that image of Jesus would have been distorted over time if artists were only copying others' images of Jesus? How could so many people hold such a similar image in their minds even though they had never actually seen him, just someone else's version? Perhaps it is subconscious memory or a spiritual connection to him that we all share.

The second aspect of the documentary that interested me was the physical timeline factor. The shroud was once tested for age using carbon dating. When the carbon test results came back, the results said that the shroud was only seven hundred years old not two thousand years old. Skeptics then dismissed the shroud as unreal. During later examination, it was shown that the test piece of fabric used for the carbon date test was from a repair patch on the shroud and was actually newer material than the shroud, so the actual age of the older material could be two thousand years old. Oops. I guess science can make mistakes and be wrong once in a while.

Now that the shroud's age was back into question, scientists were going to take a different approach to help determine the shroud's age. They used what is called the Sudarium of Oviedo.

The Sudarium of Oviedo is a small piece of fabric about eighty-four by fifty-three centimeters in size, and <u>both scientists and religious scholars</u> believe this to be the actual cloth used to clean and cover Jesus's face after his crucifixion. Unlike the shroud, the sudarium bears no imprint, but it does have blood stains.

During the show *The Real Face of Jesus*, experts compared the blood stain patterns of the sudarium with the shroud's imprint. *The match was identical.* The sudarium has been in a Spanish cathedral in Oviedo since the seventh century, which means the shroud could be from Jesus and could be two thousand years old. Between the blood stains and the age, I do believe that the shroud is real. Science could never actually prove it, because they don't have Jesus's DNA, but they also believed it to be real.

I also believe the Shroud of Turin is real because of the actual blood stains on the shroud. As I watched scientists examine this shroud and re-create the face of Jesus, they had taken the shroud and they had to separate the actual blood stains from the imprint of the body itself, which is also on the shroud. They needed to do this because the blood stains interfered and blurred the image of Jesus's face when they tried to capture the image on camera. When they had enhanced the image on the computer to make that faded imprint stand out, you could clearly see the face of Jesus with the enhancement. However, when the scientists enhanced the blood stains, I was stunned!

My heart literally stopped for a second when I watched those artists enhance the blood on Jesus's body. There before my eyes stood the crucified body of Jesus Christ! I was literally mesmerized by the sight of it and horrified at the same time. Right there, I knew I was looking at Jesus and that he had died for me and that everything was true. Right there, I knew he was real. He had died for me, and he had suffered!

It was the most brutal thing I had ever seen. That says something, when everyone reading this book knows how violent present-day movies and video games are. The manufactured violence in those films was nothing compared to what I saw when they enhanced that image. It was a picture of a man tortured to death, and I will never forget what I saw until the day I die! I could not imagine anyone enduring that type of torture, let alone my God. He had suffered horribly.

From head to toe, that image suddenly became red with his injuries. Starting at the top of his head, you could clearly see the outline of the crown of thorns. His face was bloody and beaten; the body was literally torn apart from being whipped repeatedly. You could see the lashings from head to toe. Like I said, it was one of the most brutal images I have ever seen.

You could also clearly see the wounds on his hands and feet from where he was nailed to the cross. I sat back and thought about how painful that must have been; especially when you think about what it is like just to hit your thumb with a hammer. You could also see the final wound, the spear to his side, and you could see where all the blood ran down his body from that wound. Not only did Jesus die for you, but it really was a sacrifice, because he was tortured, and he suffered.

Science and history both prove he was a real person, so why can't people believe what he said? I see people every day believing things they see and read. Why can't they believe what Jesus had to say? His message was about love and hope. **People would rather believe in nothing than something.** What other person could have endured such pain and torture? Seriously, think about the trauma that his body endured. Any normal person would have gone into shock after a beating and whipping like that! No other person could have taken such punishment, to the point where the meat was literally getting ripped from the body, unless he was the Son of God.

The next point I want to make about the shroud is about the imprint. When you look at the shroud, the imprint is faint but visible to the naked eye. The controversy with the shroud is that some people believe that the imprint itself was painted on. They believe someone, long ago, painted this image onto the shroud and then left it for us to find. Scientists examined the shroud again and again to discover the authenticity of the imprint. Although they can't conclude how the image was imprinted on the shroud, they can say with certainty that they don't believe the image was painted on or faked. Science concluded that the imprint was part of the fabric itself, part of the actual fibers, not a substance painted on. Science believes that some sort of radiation energy imposed the imprint of the person into the fabric!

The resurrection is considered to be the greatest miracle of all time, because it is when Jesus raised his physical body to heaven. The imprint on the shroud sure sounds like evidence of his resurrection, of radiation released during the resurrection. That definitely seems possible to me; after all, the shroud is real, and Jesus was real. Also, how many bodies create that much radiation? Only godly bodies could have produced such radiation. We didn't have science back then to test his body, but could he have had a special energy radiating from within? We will never know. The scientists examining the shroud say time and time again that although they can't prove the shroud was truly the shroud of Jesus, they believe the shroud is not a fake.

People reading this book are closing their minds right now when they think about a physical body rising from the dead. They probably think, "How is that possible? When you die, you're dead." Keep reading my book, because my theory addresses how I think it could have been possible. I will discuss it more in the chapter discussing matter and antimatter.

The last thing I want to say about the shroud is about how it started to make me think, and how those thoughts became this book. When I was watching those scientists separate the bloodstains from the imprint to re-create the face of Jesus, I started thinking, and my brain started turning. The graphic artists had a hard time converting the two-dimensional image from the shroud into a three-dimensional model. I like to draw, so I understood the trouble they were having trying to create this model. I have the same problem when I see something in my head and I try to draw it on a two-dimensional piece of paper. Usually the image becomes distorted and not quite what I was picturing in my head; it's the loss of that dimension that plays tricks with your mind.

These are the thoughts that started it all. The shroud got my thoughts snowballing from one thought to the next thought. All these "what-ifs" popped into my head, and the more I thought about it, the more logical everything seemed. The more I thought about it in the big picture, the more I could see all the dots fitting together. As all these thoughts started snowballing, I decided I had better start writing them down, because who knows where they could lead me. I also decided to write them down because not only did they seem logical, but they also seemed simple and plausible.

As I started thinking about the problem the graphic artists were having trying to re-create the face of Jesus, I started thinking about how our eyes are just like cameras, and how they really only see two dimensionally. Our brains just re-create that three-dimensional world, just like the artists were trying to re-create that image of Jesus. When the artists and scientists finally figured out a way to trick the camera into snapping a more three-dimensional image, the face of Jesus "popped out," and the illusion was shattered. I thought if our world is like this three-dimensional image and we are looking through our two-dimensional eyes, then how much of our world are we not seeing? We are living in one big optical illusion created by our own eyes, scientifically and biologically speaking. Our eyes can play tricks on us; we all know and can admit that. The phrase the brain sees what it wants to see is literal!

If the graphic artists can trick their cameras to see a truer three-dimensional image without distortion, then how can I do that with my eyes? I want to see the real image in front of me, not the two-dimensional trick my mind and eyes play. How can I do that? How can I see beyond my two-dimensional eyes and that flat image in front of me? I want to see the true depth of the world I live in! How can I counter that illusion? How can I see without using my physical/biological eyes? The ones that lie to me and don't show me the true world I live in? How can I do that? The rest is in my theory.

MY THEORY

My theory will be broken up into sections so you can follow along with my thought process. I am going to start by talking about how I see dimensions. This way you can get an idea of how this thought all started, and from there I will tie everything together.

DIMENSIONS

I have always had a hard time visualizing dimensions in my head, especially when I first heard about them and tried to understand the concept. I had always imagined this invisible universe in my head that was the other dimension, until I started to really read and try to understand dimensions from a physical/biological point of view. Up to this point, I had always thought of dimensions like heaven and hell—I thought of them spiritually. When all these thoughts started snowballing, I ended up adding a more physical and biological point of view to my understanding of dimensions.

OK, this is going to be hard to explain, but I am going to try my best. I started thinking, we have two-dimensional eyes, and we live in a three-dimensional world. We can move left to right, front to back, and we can go up and down. But then I really started thinking of the biological aspect of it. We are dimensional beings. Our bodies hold volume, they are not flat, and our universe is dimensional. You cannot occupy the same point in space as I do without moving me out of the way and into a different geographical point in space. So with that in mind, I started thinking deeper. If we are dimensional beings and time is a dimension, we naturally seem to progress through dimensions as we grow and age naturally throughout our life.

This is how I came up with my own dimension level system that I will illustrate by example, but first I want to explain it.

I consider my soul or spirit to be dimension level zero: it has no physical volume, and it is an entity, so I consider it to be zero-dimensional. When we are conceived and created as a physical being inside the womb, I consider this dimension level one. You are now a dimensional being. When you are born and you open your eyes to see the world around you, you are still too small to crawl or move; but you use your eyes and grow to dimension level two, because the only world you know is the one you can see with your two-dimensional eyes. As you grow, you learn to crawl and walk, you discover your three-dimensional world around you, and you progress to dimension level three. Remember, you are not changing dimensions, just progressing through dimension LEVELS. You are still just a physical being that can occupy only one point in space at a time.

So as you grow, age, and explore your three-dimensional world throughout your life, you travel through the fourth dimension level: time.

I do believe there are more dimension levels that we will discover throughout our existence as time continues to progress and we grow as a species, not as individuals. I think more dimension levels could be out there, but I really think it's also a parallel universe that's out there! I think it's that invisible parallel universe that you are in when you are in zero dimension level or spirit level. If you have zero dimensions and are an entity, anything could be possible out there in space, or here on earth for that matter. If you have zero dimensions, you would have no physical mass to see; you would be invisible like spirits or souls! This is what started my whole theory and the snowball effect! If you had no dimension and zero mass, and simply consisted of your spirit or soul, could you move at light speed? If travel at light speed is possible, then that makes exploring our universe to the edges possible!

Now that I have given you a basic idea of how I see dimensions and dimension levels, you can look at the example I have given to help with the visual aspect of my idea. The concept of dimension levels is integral to my theory. I just wanted to explain it to you first, before I started talking about the really deep parts of my theory. I also realize that my idea of dimensions and dimension levels is based on the belief that I have a soul or spirit, and that I also tried to account for the biological part of myself. Like I said earlier, I believe the universe is alive and biological, since life exists, and I believe there is a spiritual realm in the universe. So my idea of dimensions and dimension levels does have three aspects: physical, biological, and spiritual.

This is an example of how I view dimensions visually.

Dimensions

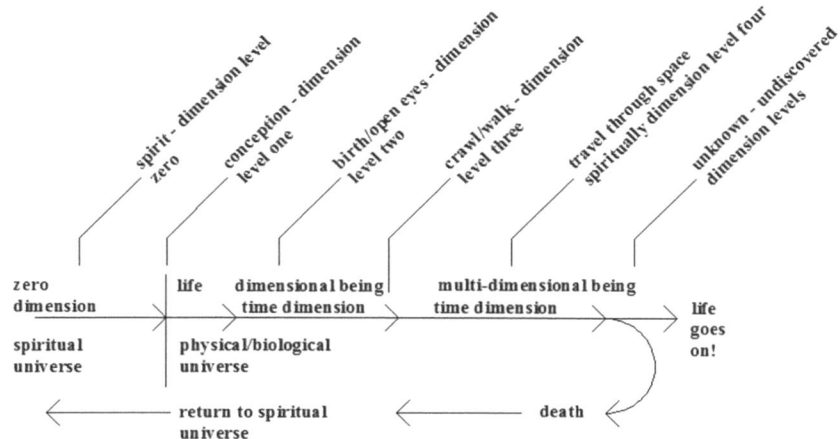

This is how I think dimensions and dimension levels could work in relation to both a physical/biological and an invisible parallel universe. Now that you understand this, you will understand what I am talking about when I refer back to dimension levels throughout the book.

I believe there is life out in space like aliens, but also spirits in a different dimension level or parallel universe, and that's why we have not found any life out in space yet. I think the way to travel through space is through our brains and spirits. So that's where I am going to begin.

THE BRAIN

Everyone knows the brain is capable of amazing things, but I want to share a few basic facts about the brain before we start. I am obviously not a brain surgeon, so I am going to keep it simple.

I know the brain has over one hundred billion neurons and that neurons are cell-like and contain a nucleus. A nucleus contains DNA, the blueprint for who you are as an individual. Neurons are what make your brain function and also give you your thinking capability. They also keep your physical body functioning by controlling your nervous system and subconscious. There are different neurons for different brain functions.

Neurons are basically electrical relays that send charges back and forth at designated times to communicate between the nervous system and the brain, or between parts of the brain. There are also special sensory neurons to activate our senses and how we PERCEIVE our senses. What would happen if your brain relays were set wide open like a car throttle, or if you could gain control of your neurons? Do we have neurons in our brains that trigger senses we did not yet know our brains could even register?

People think that you only use 10 percent of your brain, but that is actually untrue. It turns out your brain is active all the time. Yes, it rests when you sleep, but it is still active. You do dream, and you are still alive and breathing. What effects does zero gravity have on neurons in space? Has anyone ever studied the brain under a heavy meditative state while in space under zero gravity conditions? Could we eject our consciousness out of our body by controlling our brain, to have a controlled, out-of-body experience? Could you create a wormhole with your brain? The point I am really trying to get at is this: if our brains are so active, could our ability to unlock something special really be just lack of brain control on our part? Could we learn to control our spiritual selves, to train our brains through focus and meditation?

The reason why I think the brain and the spirit are the key to space travel is this: in order to do any real travel through space, we are going to need to travel at the speed of light. Even at the particle level, when traveling at or near the speed of light, the mass expands, causing resistance and slowing it down, which means you need even more energy to keep moving. Now I will get into this a little more for people so they understand Einstein's theory and what I am getting at later on in the chapter. To summarize; I think the brain and spirit are the key to space travel because if you are a spirit or an entity, you have no mass and therefore can travel at the speed of light easier, because you are not physical. The less mass you have to send somewhere, the less energy you will need to send it there.

Regarding the brain, I want to point out how special neurons are since they contain our DNA, and that your brain and neurons together create your physical awareness. I think the consciousness is the physical part of our spirit, the link between this universe and the invisible parallel universe that I think is out there for the spiritual part of us.

EINSTEIN'S THEORY OF RELATIVITY

I have always been fascinated with Einstein and what he has managed to figure out about our universe. Whenever I had tried to understand Einstein's theory, it had always seemed too confusing, especially when people started talking about time as a dimension. I could never grasp that concept until I really started to try to understand Einstein and his theory on a simple level. I am going to go back over the basic concept to make it simple for people reading this book. That way, they will understand how I fit it into my theory. I will go over the theory very simply and explain it the way that I learned it when I first understood the concept for myself. Hopefully that will help others understand it as well. Please refer back to the examples below as I explain how I think Einstein's theory works.

Einstein says if you are motionless in space and travel in the time (x) direction at the speed of light, space (y) will contract or shorten, making it easier to reach the edges of space.

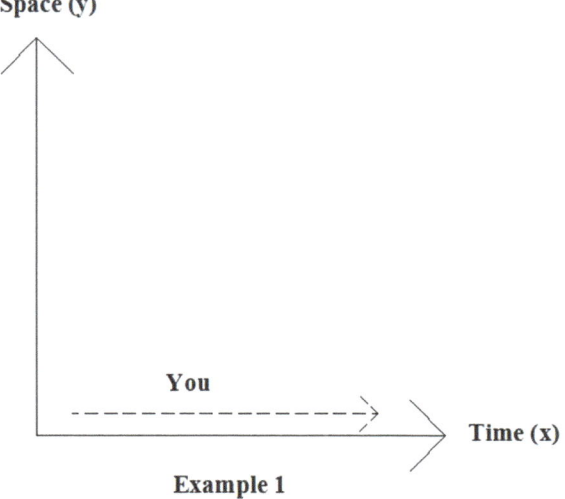

Example 1

As you start moving toward the space (y) direction, you will start to lose time (x). See the example below.

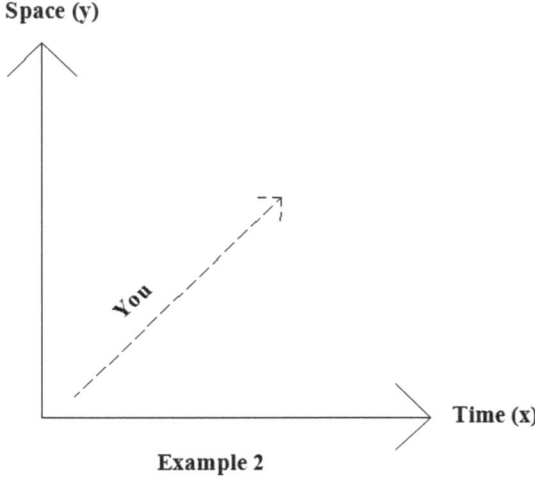

Example 2

As you continue to head toward the space direction at the speed of light and continue to lose time (x), you will eventually stop time if you head directly into the space (y) direction. See the example below.

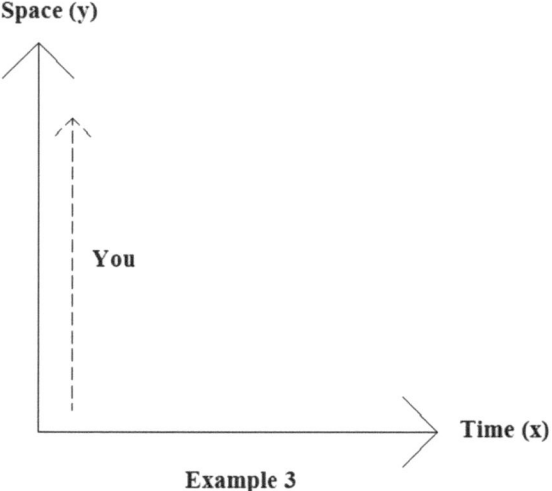

Example 3

Einstein's Theory of Relativity

In theory, if you were motionless in space and traveled in the space (y) direction, time should be stopped if you traveled through space at the speed of light. Theoretically, the trip would be instantaneous to you if time was stopped. Remember, it's all relative to you as the observer.

Now this is the problem I have with the modern space program and our approach to Einstein's theory. They say that for his theory to work, you have to start off by being **motionless**. How can you become motionless in this universe? Can you ever really become motionless in space? How can you become motionless if you are on a planet that rotates on its own axis at a thousand miles per hour? Everything in the universe is in motion—from our own planet's spinning to our planet's revolution around our sun at sixty-seven thousand miles per hour! Our solar system exists in our galaxy, the Milky Way, and that's in motion, too. How can we ever even start Einstein's theory and become motionless in this universe?

To me, this means that anything that has physical mass will always be in motion in the universe, and we will never find a motionless spot. We need to stop thinking so physical! My thought is this: if I want to become motionless in this universe, I need to use the part of myself that has no mass and make it perfectly still. The only part of me that has zero mass, but is still me, is my spirit and consciousness! That means I need to make my physical consciousness (my brain) still, and then my soul will be motionless in the universe and still contain zero mass. If you travel without mass, you will not slow down when you travel at the speed of light. Could you travel at light speed through the universe as a consciousness, leaving your physical body back here on earth? It would still be you, your spirit and consciousness, but your physical body would remain on earth during an out-of-body experience.

I think that makes more sense than trying to build some giant rocket ship to survive the speed of light, especially if we can't even get a particle to travel that fast without expanding. Even if we could build the ship to go that fast, could we protect our physical bodies well enough to travel at that speed? Think of the force you would endure!

I don't think our physical bodies are meant to travel in space. I think that's why we can't survive physically out in space. I see it as one big hint. I think the life out in space is not physical; it's spiritual! I think maybe the physical life that might be out there is hidden from our two-dimensional eyes, and that's why we can't find it: we are meant NOT to find it. I think we are meant to live our own lives and figure out why WE are here.

Now we need to talk more about Einstein's theory and TIME. People disregard God, because they use time as a factor. I want to say, in my eyes, time is irrelevant! Time is affected by motion or speed. The GPS satellites we use every day in our cars have clocks on them that run faster than clocks on earth! Einstein proves time fluctuates depending on where you are as the observer. So if time can fluctuate depending on where you are in the universe, how can science and religion even try to compare timelines? If the universe is in constant motion and has been since the dawn of time, and time can fluctuate, how can you even begin to compare evolution vs. religion? Einstein says both time and space can be manipulated. His time dilation and space contraction theories are proven, so why can't it be God who performed these feats like creating our physical universe with the big bang and setting life into motion? Do we not believe him because we can't see him? It could definitely make the story of Genesis in the Bible true, and also the creation of man, even if we did evolve.

> **Then the lord God formed a man from the dust of the ground and breathed into his nostrils the breath of life, and the man became a living being. (Genesis 2:7, New International Version)**

> **And the dust returns to the earth as it was, and the spirit returns to the God who gave it. (Ecclesiastes 12:7, English Standard Version)**

Remember, the greatest thinkers in the world once thought our earth was flat. Someone had to come along and challenge that idea! Now I don't claim to have answers, like I said, just ideas, but I want to challenge what we believe and not leave any possibilities out, including God.

We also have to consider the fact that our whole universe is expanding out from itself. That right; there is a constant fluctuation of time. If you identify point A and point B and then time yourself to see how long it takes to cover that distance, then do the same experiment with the two points expanding away from each other, you will get a different result. How can time ever be a consideration if it's constantly changing? What if you were an entity like God and were already at both points A and B? Time cannot exist, so time is not a factor with God. God is everywhere! So if Einstein says time fluctuation is possible for us to achieve, why couldn't God achieve it? That solves the whole time debate to me! We have to remember the only real constant in the universe is the speed of light; that's the only thing that stays the same. Time and space are both just variables that can be changed.

To me, it seems that the key to space travel is becoming motionless! I also think science was on the right track; they went as small as they could with particles, but that mass is still too big. They need to get smaller or lose mass altogether and use something that has zero mass. I think the brain and spirit could do both of those things if we experimented with them and believed!

I also like to keep in mind one of the greatest thinkers of all time, Isaac Newton, who said: "for every action there is an equal and opposite reaction." If I have a physical body that was created, then I must have a spiritual one. I just like to remind people reading this book of that! What sounds crazier: that we need to figure out how to build rockets and protective gear to find God or whatever is out there; or that God created the vessel within us, and it's been there all along? Honestly, my soul sounds like the perfect vessel for me to travel the universe. I would certainly protect my body if I could just leave it here! If my soul and consciousness could have zero mass and I could achieve motionlessness, then this sounds to me like the perfect recipe to execute Einstein's theory, or at least a good starting point!

Before working my way toward the next part of my theory, let's review the basics of Einstein's theory.

To make Einstein's theory work, we have to be motionless. I believe we will never really achieve this, because our entire universe is in motion physically. So instead of starting out in examples one and three, we are really starting out in example two. I think it's that physical motion of the universe itself that will keep us from truly achieving light speed.

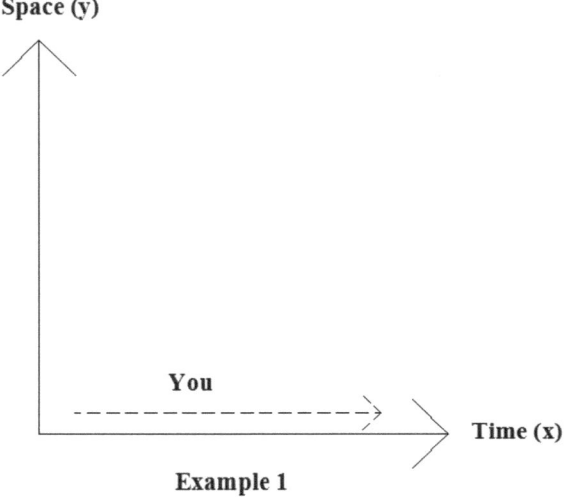

Example 1

Because of that motion, I think we are failing without even realizing it. I think motion is making space and time fluctuate back and forth on us, and that's why we need to be motionless. The modern space program is trying to travel that direction now (example three) and trying to go faster to achieve light speed. If we could achieve light speed, time would stop for us, and we could travel those light years without time passing right?

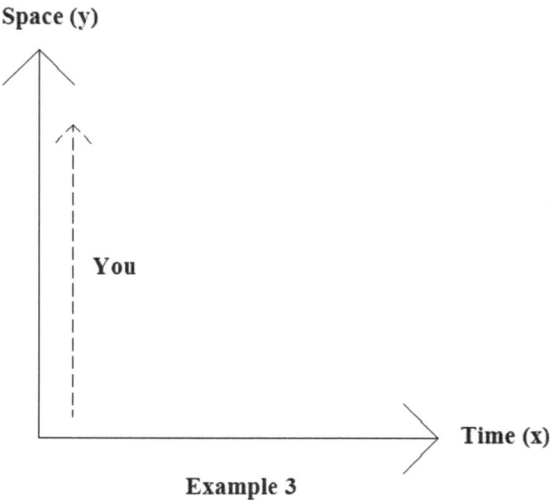

Example 3

I honestly don't think we are meant to travel the time direction. I don't think we are meant to mess with time or our futures/destinies. That's why the grandfather paradox exists. If you went back in time to kill your grandfather and you succeeded in killing him, then how could you ever be born? If you never could exist, how could you go back and shoot him? It's a paradox. I don't think time was meant to be messed with; that's why I think we are on the right track with example three and going up the space direction.

I believe there is definitely something to meditation, or people would not have practiced it for thousands of years. They say it makes your consciousness still. I personally have not been that successful yet at trying to calm my brain into total stillness. I have tried but need more practice; my brain just runs too fast; perhaps I should say that it's not properly trained.

Just because we have not unlocked something special during meditation does not mean it's not there. Just because no one else has ever figured it out while practicing meditation for thousands of years does not mean it's not there; maybe there is just more to it! I do personally believe part of the key to figuring out space travel and what is out there is in the brain and meditation. I think maybe it's the first part of controlling our consciousness or spirit in order to travel through space and have a controlled out-of-body experience. Yes, I believe in God and think he does exist, but who knows what we would encounter if we were able to create controlled out-of-body experiences! I believe in our parallel (opposite) universe, our spiritual one! We have a physical universe, why not a spiritual one? Every action has an equal and opposite reaction in this universe. If a physical universe was created, why couldn't a spiritual universe have been created as well?

I do believe science is on the right track (sort of); I just wish they would stop being so physical all the time and add some biological and spiritual aspects into the equations. Biology does exist, and spirits and spiritual worlds could exist, so why exclude them from possibilities?

Now I could spend this whole book talking about different ideas about how to try to make Einstein's theory work or which direction we should traveling, but I don't know the answers. I just have had some ideas. But there are two things I do want to say about his theory. First,

I think that being motionless seems to be the key, and I don't think we will ever physically achieve it. Second, mass seems to be the other problem. No matter how small we go physically, it just expands and gains mass near light speed and slows down. We need something without physical mass—an entity!

Now that you know basically how Einstein's theory works and how I understand his theory, I want to talk a little bit more about how I see God, life, science, and evolution. Bear with me if I repeat something; it's only so I can start jumping from some of those thoughts to new ones. I repeat so that I can show you the connections.

When I sit back and think about the human species, evolution, and religion, it really gets my brain going. I do believe in the concept of evolution; like I said before, it wouldn't be a good design on God's part if we could not evolve and grow with our environment. When I think about evolution, though, some things just don't fit. As a species, we have not really evolved to fit with our environment like animals do. We have only really evolved in our brains and in our posture. We don't continue to grow and evolve to fit naturally with the earth so we can live naturally with the environment, or is it just our mentality and the way we think as a species?

When I look at evolution from a biological standpoint, I have questions. First, why have our five senses not evolved and improved? When we look at animals in nature and their senses, they make ours look pitiful. Why haven't our senses improved over time? The only things that have improved for humanity are our intellectual ability, our skeletal posture, and our physical facial features. I think human posture and physical beautify have evolved, but they have literally evolved from lust. The strongest and biggest of early man got to breed with the prettiest of early woman, or the one he found most physically attractive (lust). The smartest people also learned how to survive and breed, and so they too passed on their brains and thinking ability. So yes, I do believe humans have evolved with time, but perhaps not as much as we could have.

This is the point where I believe God has control of us. Why don't we have better vision and better hearing like animals do? Why are our senses so weak? Why hasn't our skin evolved to better suit our natural environment? I believe God has made us in his image, and we are actually more spiritual creatures. I think we are more spiritual than we realize and that is why we don't evolve to naturally fit into this environment; we are not meant to evolve with this environment.

> ***Then God said, "Let us make mankind in our image, in our likeness, so that they may rule over the fish in the sea and the birds in the sky, over the livestock and all the wild animals, and over all the creatures that move along the ground." So God created mankind in his own image, in the image of God he created them, male and female he created them. (Genesis 1:26–27, New International Version)***

I do believe in evolution to a certain degree, but I think the animals were created by God to be able to evolve and adapt to their environment, while humankind evolves more spiritually and intellectually. We do grow and evolve physically and biologically to a degree, but our evolution is more intellectual and spiritual. God does not really care about our physical bodies; he knows they die. He is worried with our spiritual bodies. He keeps our physical bodies alive because he has to, so we can find him.

We grow as perfect as a seed can grow into a tree—from an egg to a person. For the miracle of life to exist, two special cells must meet, be protected, then combine and grow to produce that special life. This needs to happen twice in nature: once to create the male and once to create the female, and then you will have the start of a species. In all the random chaos in nature, could all this coincidence and creation of life really happen on its own? Yes, of course it *could* happen, and so it is possible. But couldn't God just have just decided to make it easy and create life with a miracle? Yes, I think that is also possible. Think of all the unique species of life out there, could we really have evolved off of each other when the first cells developed?

If we can grow and evolve physically and biologically not only as individuals but as a species, why can't we grow and evolve both individually and as a species spiritually? Is it because we can only see our physical bodies and not our spirits? Look at your three-dimensional universe with your simple two-dimensional eyes! Remember that your brain creates the image of the three-dimensional world you *think* you live in; just because you can't see that other universe or dimension level does not mean it does not exist. Your brain sees what it wants to see!

Forever Always by Octavio Ocampo

Spirit of the Woods by Sandro Del Prete

An example of a Penrose triangle using dice

Calvary by Octavio Ocampo

If the brain sees what it wants to see, then we can't trust our physical eyes! Our two-dimensional eyes have been creating that constant optical illusion since the moment we opened them. **Our eyes create** *that flat two-dimensional image, and our brain fills in the depth with what it thinks it should see. What a great place to hide God, right in front of our eyes!* Knowing we can't trust our physical eyes and that they can deceive us, we have to admit our world could be filled with volume that we just can't see physically. Does a spiritual universe still sound crazy? What about having a soul? If it does not sound so crazy anymore, why couldn't we use our brains and spirits together to try and travel the universe?

I do believe I have that spirit alive inside me that could do these things, if I could just figure out the trick. But in saying that, I believe I have that soul alive inside me. I am saying that I believe God created me and gave me my spirit just like the Bible says he did.

> *Then the lord God formed the man of dust from the ground and breathed into his nostrils the breath of life, and the man became a living creature. (Genesis 2:7, English Standard Version)*

If I believe my spirit is alive within me and that my body is just the vessel of the spirit, then I must believe that when I die, it is only my physical body that dies. My spirit will remain alive and go somewhere.

> *And the dust returns to the earth as it was, and the spirit returns to God who gave it. (Ecclesiastes 12:7, English Standard Version)*

It sure sounds like a simple enough lifecycle to me, and doesn't the simplest explanation tend to be the right one?

I know I have that spirit that is alive inside me for a few reasons. I am going to bring up a few more points for people who think their spirit is really just consciousness created by neurons. When I have a headache, my head physically throbs, but when I see my daughter hurt, I hurt inside myself; the pain is nowhere near my head. If a thought causes me this pain, why do I feel it deep inside myself by my heart?

If I love someone and that person dies, it's not my leg or arm muscles that hurt, or my brain for that matter. My brain does not feel compassion for someone who needs help. I feel compassion near my heart. If these feelings were simply neuron-generated, then I would feel them in my head, not my soul!

The reason I discussed the soul at such length is because it ties into the next aspect of my theory: near-death and out-of-body experiences.

NEAR-DEATH AND OUT-OF-BODY EXPERIENCES

Nearly everyone has heard of near-death and out-of-body experiences. I have been fascinated by stories of near-death experiences and have read a number of books on them. Anyone who has read these experiences will all say the same thing: most of the details are fairly consistent.

During this next phase of the book, keep my theory (as much as we have addressed it so far) in the back of your mind. Remember that I think we have souls and that I believe we can use our brains to travel the universe.

The most common aspect of near-death stories is the light. People usually say there is a white light or that they travel through tunnels of white light. The Bible says God is the light. People say they experience a "popping" sensation, a separation from their bodies. In this separation, they describe becoming like entities looking down on their bodies. People have described these experiences so vividly and claim they felt as real as the physical world. Aside from these details, the stories differ slightly depending on individual experience. If you take the time to read some of the stories, you'll see just how many little details these stories have in common.

If you can just "pop" out of your dimensional body, then common sense tells me you would become a dimensionless or zero-dimensional being. You would also become multi-dimensional because your body would be at one point in space and your spirit or consciousness would be at another dimension in space.

It's All Relative... The God Factor...

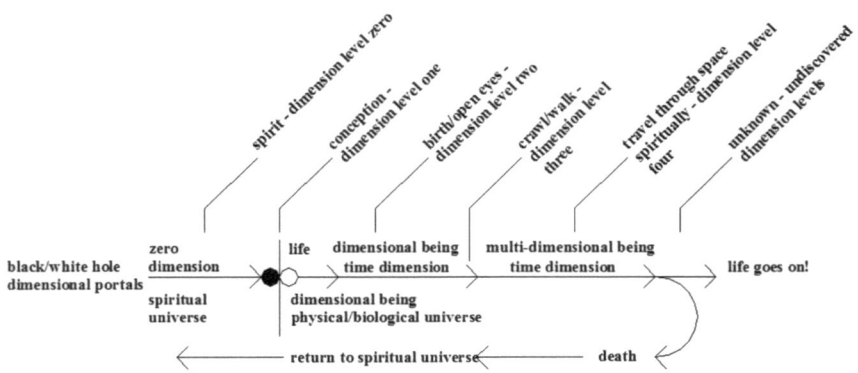

Those near-death experience stories reveal a few truths. The first is that when I do die, I will go somewhere. Secondly, these stories tell me that it is possible to separate your soul/spiritual body from your physical/biological body and still remain connected while the physical body stays alive.

I know that during a near-death experience the physical body experiences severe trauma and usually almost dead (hence the name). Now think about what an out-of-body experience is; is it the same thing as a near-death experience but without the physical trauma? I have never experienced either, but common sense makes this inference.

People describe seeing dead relatives and Jesus during near-death experiences. Does it really sound crazy to think when you die and your physical body dies (and you go from dimensional to zero-dimensional), that your spirit lives and you just becomes an entity? That does not sound crazy to me at all; in fact it makes sense to me. If our physical bodies live in a physical world, why can't our spiritual selves live in a spiritual world aka heaven? Again, this sounds perfectly possible to me. Jesus was a real person who died just like us; why does it sound so crazy that he would be in that spiritual world with the other spirits? Why do countless people who have near-death experiences say they have seen Jesus?

These near-death experiences sound just like Einstein's theory of relativity happening to me. It sounds just like what I was describing in example three, using your spirit to travel in the space (y) direction. You would be a motionless, zero-dimensional (zero mass) entity who could travel through space or the (y) direction at the speed of light.

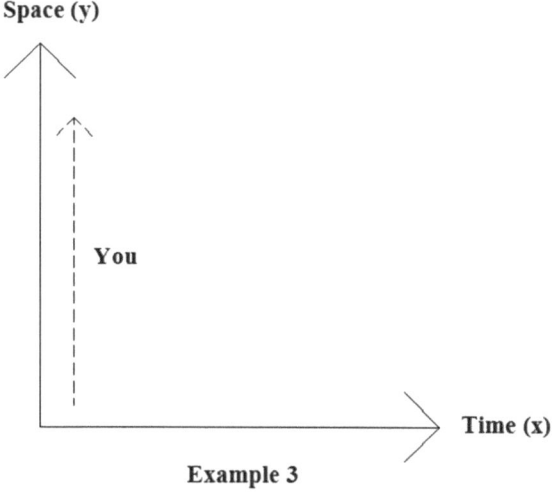

Example 3

This is why I think we could use our spirits or souls to travel through space. If we could learn to first separate our souls from our physical bodies, I think we could control them consciously with our minds to travel our physical universe. That's why I am so interested in out-of-body experiences.

What would we find if we could create and control our own out-of-body experiences, so that we could project our souls out of our bodies while retaining a conscious connection to them? What would we see if we could project ourselves out beyond what we can see with our two-dimensional eyes? Imagine if you could project your spirit across the universe to different planets using only your mind, all while keeping your physical body and brain back here on earth.

As I have said before, I am not a brain surgeon or astrophysicist, so I don't know how everything works, but I like to think it could be possible. The brain is an amazing and powerful thing. It uses light energy to function—the one constant in the universe. They say our eyes are the windows to our soul; is the brain the doorway to our soul?

Let's talk a little more about near-death and out-of-body experiences. I believe each type of experience has its purpose. I think near-death experiences allow people to come back from death and share their knowledge of the afterlife with the living. I think the out-of-body experiences allow us to learn how to travel through space and the universe.

As I said before, most retellings of near-death experiences that I have read about share the same details: a trip to heaven or hell and interaction with other spirits. In heaven, people see dead relatives and other angels; in hell people see souls burning in a pit of fire. People have believed in an afterlife of some sort across cultures throughout history. It just can't be a coincidence that so many near-death experiences are so similar despite divides of culture and time.

If nature, life, and the universe are so random, how come we don't hear random, conflicting stories during peoples' near-death experiences? Why don't I hear stories of people traveling to other solar systems or galaxies? Why don't I hear stories about people meeting aliens or moving on to their next life? Or is heaven the other universe you travel to, the parallel to our physical universe? Remember, every action has an equal and opposite reaction. If a physical universe was created, a spiritual one could also have been created. Perhaps instead of meeting aliens, maybe we're meant to encounter our dead relatives in spiritual form? How about next lives or reincarnation? Isn't moving from a physical/biological form to a spiritual one a form of reincarnation? It is the end of your physical/biological life and the beginning of a new spiritual one. That sure sounds like reincarnation to me.

Both nature and the universe are not as random as we think; perhaps nature and the universe itself were perfectly created. I see too many similarities for everything in the universe to be random. Perhaps we are overthinking the concept of the universe. Perhaps everything is a lot simpler and more obvious than we realize. Maybe the whole key to the universe is God, and that's why science can't finish the puzzle.

That's why I think near-death experiences are visions of heaven and the afterlife. They allow the living to know it's out there, and then we can believe in it without fear. This is God's way of showing us not to be afraid. How else could he tell us what's out there? He has been showing himself to us all along. People always ask why God does not show him-

Near-Death and Out-of-Body Experiences

self if he exists, and yet that's exactly what he does through near-death experiences.

During near-death experiences, I think our spirits travel to heaven and back as a zero-dimensional entity at the speed of light. This is similar to the third example of how I think Einstein's theory works; yes, his theory works physically, but can't it also work spiritually?

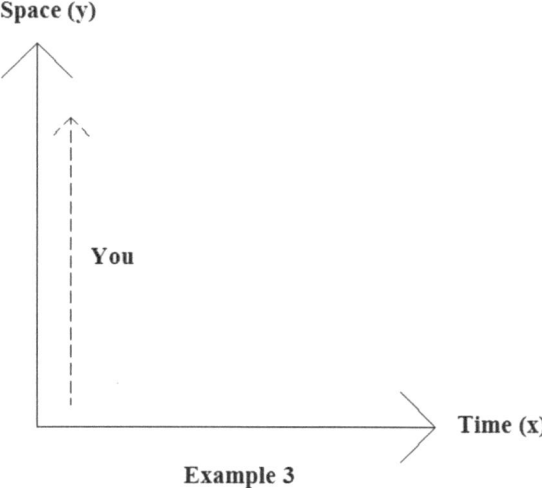

Example 3

And the dust returns to the ground it came from, and the spirit returns to the God who gave it. (Ecclesiastes 12:7, English Standard Version)

I want to talk some more about out-of-body experiences. I have not heard very many firsthand accounts of out-of-body experiences, but I have heard a couple. My grandmother's experience was particularly interesting to me, especially because she is also a very religious person who believes in God and heaven.

I have only heard her story twice in my life: I first heard it when I was about twelve, and I heard it again last week. I didn't remember many details after the first time I heard the story; I was a kid and hadn't really paid attention. I do remember her making a big deal about it, though.

I was between ten and twelve, and my brothers and I were staying with my dad for the summer, and he lived with my grandma. I remember her lying down on the floor in the den like she does every day, to stretch out her legs and back and just relax for about fifteen or thirty minutes. My brothers and I were outside playing in the yard while she was lying down, and when we came in later on, she was awake and excited by what she'd just experienced.

She had told us about a "vision-like experience" she'd had while taking her nap. She was so excited. It seemed like she told the story over and over, but I was only twelve or so and didn't really care about the details or the significance of what she was saying. I remember her saying something about seeing a vision of the future and her saying she had a sort of vision of all her kids and grandkids grown up! Later, I realized she must have had an out-of-body experience, but I never asked her about it again.

Honestly, I didn't want to know how my future was supposedly going to turn out. It was like sealing my fate. If I didn't know how it was going to turn out, then the possibilities were endless. It was like knowing my future would seal my destiny. I just did not want to know. So I never asked her about her experience until about a week ago.

During the process of writing this book and before I got a chance to go talk with my grandma about her experience, my grandpa happened to pass away. He was my grandma's ex-husband. To give you a sense of their relationship, I could just describe it as hatred, but that would not actually do it justice. To put it simply, I am thirty-three years old now, and I have never seen them together even once! They were divorced long before I was born, and there was a bad blood between the two sides of the family ever since. And, yes, I am sharing this information for a reason.

When I went to talk to my grandma about her experience, I got to hear more from her than I ever imagined.

When I walked into her house, she immediately knew something was unusual. She noticed my notebook, and she kept asking me why I had just stopped over. Even though I spend quite a bit of time with her, she knew something was different. I told her I had started writing my book and that I wanted to ask her some questions about her out-of-body experience, the one she had told us about when I was a kid. I will be honest; I felt a little strange going up and just asking her this out of the blue, especially since she had never again brought it up.

I began telling my grandma about my book and why I had wanted to hear about her experience. My grandma looked at me and said, "Let me tell you what happened last week! It happened the morning that your grandpa died." She definitely got my attention. The morning my grandpa passed away, she was sleeping; it was still very early. She said that she could actually feel someone looking at her while she was sleeping, and that's what started to wake her up. She said she felt a presence near her, as though someone were standing very close. When she opened her eyes, she saw my grandpa standing right in front of her! She said he had looked young, like he had in his prime. He didn't look anything like the old man she'd seen in our photographs from the funeral I went to. He then tried to reach out and hug her, and she said it felt real enough, and she was awake enough to sit up in bed. Then it was over, and he was gone. A moment later, my aunt, who was staying with my grandma, received a call saying that grandpa was taken to the hospital and was in bad shape. However, we did not think he was going to pass away that morning. My grandmother encountered him in the very early morning, and he passed away at about 10:00 a.m.

Interestingly, relatives later told me that my grandpa said my grandma's name in the hospital that morning. Now I am not sure of the actual timing of these events, but they definitely occurred within a few hours of one another, if not a few minutes. Was my grandpa in the in-between world—still physically in this world but so close to death that his spirit had separated from his body? It sounded to me like my grandpa was having the out-of-body/near-death experience, and my grandma was still psychologically and cosmically connected to him. It was as though he was trying to say good-bye one last time and make amends before he moved off into the spirit world.

I find it very strange that all this happened at the same time, that my grandma could have such a strange spiritual experience with my grandpa, who she has not seen in over thirty years, the very morning of his death. Now my grandma really had my mind going, and she hadn't yet told me the experience I was initially interested in.

The second story was the one that happened to her when I was about twelve, the one I remember but don't remember. My grandma let me tell her what I had remembered about the story first, and then she shared her own memory of the experience. I was right when I said she was lying down on the floor as usual with her feet up in the air, stretching out her legs and back. She said she was lying there thinking about her father who had passed away when she was young. She was sort of praying and just thinking about all her troubles and talking to him in her own way, since he was dead.

As she was laying there on the floor, she said she had this strange sensation wash over her, and when she had opened her eyes, her father, grandfather, and uncle were standing in front of her. She told me that she had recognized all three clearly: her dad, his dad, and his brother, who had been killed during World War II. She remembered seeing them in what she described as a fog-like realm, and she remembered her father communicating with her.

She said he didn't speak with words, but waves of information just started coming to her, wave after wave of thoughts. Her father had told her things about the future of her property (that's what she was worrying about at the time). She told me that everything did work out just as he told her it would. She did not really share too many specific details with me, but the one strange thing that she kept saying was that she thought I was meant to write this book. What I did not tell her, however, was how I felt that since I was meant to write this book, like I said in the beginning, then someone out there must be meant to read it.

I don't know if she had a true out-of-body experience or more of a vision. It is strange how a lot of people do feel like we have some sort of slight psychic power or sixth sense. Maybe there is more to psychic power than we realize. I definitely believe my grandma had those visions and that they were real. Could she have been in a meditative trance and made some sort of connection with her brain to the other side? I definitely think the idea of God and heaven is more possible than crazy! I do admit that both of my grandmother's experiences could have been dreams. But I don't believe that's what happened. I was with her after her first experience, and I remember her reaction and excitement.

So now that you have heard the quick versions of her stories, I want to point out a few things that I noticed. The first experience occurred when she was relaxing normally. She was not trying to sleep but was thinking deeply; she happened to be thinking about her problems at the time. She entered into a meditative state. Also, that when she was lying down, she had her feet pointed in the air; could this have caused an excess of blood and oxygen to rush to her head, leading to the visions? Did she give herself a red out? A red out is the opposite of a black out and occurs when blood rushes toward your head, not away from it. I do believe she experienced a vision and not a hallucination because of what she saw. She saw three dead relatives that were all in her father's blood line; these were not random people. In her second vision, she saw her ex-husband the very morning of his death. That seems too powerful to be a simple coincidence.

Maybe the whole key to space travel is to learn to travel with our souls, but that will never happen unless we first believe we have a soul to travel with. Maybe that's why we seem so close yet so far away as a human species. I think space and time are not meant to be travelled physical, only spiritually.

Could you stimulate an out-of-body experience if you could get your brain to fire neurons at the speed of light through concentration? Unlike meditation, which slows and stills the brain, could concentration supercharge your brain to fire neurons at light speed?

I want to get back to talking about the brain a little more before I move on to what I would call "Part B" of my theory. I consider my brain to be the "being" part of myself, at least the physical "being" part of myself. I think the brain connects our consciousness to our souls. I think everyone would agree that our souls and consciousness make us who we are. I can live without my arm, but I can't live without my brain even though both are physical/biological parts of me. So if my brain is what actually makes the physical part of "me," then why can't that be the part of me that travels through space (my consciousness)? Why does it have to be my arms, legs and physical body?

If my physical body can move through space, why can't my consciousness and soul move through space? My brain and my soul make "me," not my arms and legs. Einstein says the theory is possible; is there any reason I have to take my physical body? The more physical mass I have to move, the more velocity/speed I will need in order to reach the speed of light. To me it seems more logical to try to figure out a way to travel with my soul and consciousness instead of my physical body.

Since I believe that my brain is the link that connects my physical/biological consciousness to my soul; I think the brain is what gives my soul its character through choices I make. The brain gives my soul its physical awareness and keeps me alive. We are physical and can die since we are also biological. My brain makes the choices I encounter in life; my soul becomes the character made by those choices. I believe there is a separate part of me in there somewhere, an entity locked inside my physical brain. It's a part of my brain that is separate from the biological part that only worries about keeping itself alive. That physical/biological part of my brain will die with the rest of my body, but my character and consciousness will be one with my soul and will move on when I die.

Again, I am not a neurosurgeon, but I do know that my brain is like a natural supercomputer. The brain processes millions of bits of information back and forth. These bits of information are our neurons, little impulses of light and energy. Now I want to point out that they say the speed of light is the only constant in the universe, and our brain is basically made out of it. Einstein bases his theory of relativity on the speed of light. Light is our one constant in the universe.

Time is a variable and can change depending on your position of observation. Remember, the clocks on our GPS satellites run faster in space than our clocks here on earth. The magnetism from earth's gravity alters the clocks' speed. We are made biologically with magnetic energy. Our cells are made out of molecules, which are made out of atoms. Atoms contain protons, neutrons, and electrons. All our physical bodies are made out of are these three natural energies.

Could we alter our natural magnetism to make our neurons travel faster in our brains? Everything in our universe is basically made out of these same building blocks, including our own brains, so why couldn't it be possible to connect mentally with the universe? Could you use magnetism to push or force your neurons faster in your brain, to get your neurons to fire at light speed? I would like to think it possible, since it does not sound impossible. This idea is no crazier than trying to build a rocket to send my body at light speed!

Let's also remember that our neurons contain our DNA, and DNA makes us who we are. With that logic in mind, if DNA makes me who I am, and it's in my neurons which create my thoughts, wouldn't the two combined create my consciousness? If DNA can clone a physical/biological replica of me, why couldn't DNA from my neurons replicate my inner consciousness for an artificial out-of-body experience?

A few months ago, I was watching a show on aliens on the Discovery Channel, and this scientist was explaining his theory on aliens and DNA. He was saying how they thought a message from space could come as a biological form and the message would/could be encoded on DNA. Now, if aliens could send us a message like that, why couldn't God or the universe send a message like that to us? Encoded in our own DNA, a hidden message sent to us that we have not yet discovered. Why couldn't that be possible? Maybe we are the aliens and God is sending the messages to us.

Remember *Occam's razor—the principal that in explaining a thing, NO MORE ASSUMPTIONS should be made than are necessary.*

I want to be the first to say this: I think we will end up finding the key to the universe in a pattern found in nature or life itself.

We look at the universe as this dead, empty object, but the universe is alive! There is life everywhere; Earth is proof! So if the universe is alive, then it is a creature or being. To me, God is the living universe; I am living IN God! Look at all the opposites in nature. If the universe is alive, then I believe it has its own form of communication; it just can't speak physically but biologically or visually. Opposites are a visual form of simple math, but instead of 1+1=2, it's a matter of black and white or positives (+) and negatives (-). I think our universe is talking to us; we just need to learn how to read it, and then decode it.

For every action, there is an equal and opposite reaction
—Isaac Newton

MY THEORY (PART B)
Is God A Universal Brain?

I personally believe God is like a "big, universal brain" that guides our universe. This is my personal opinion. ***Now, if I had to try to describe God and then think of him in a more physical and scientific way, this is exactly how I would describe him.*** *I think of God as a universal entity who is alive and who created and controls the universe.*

I think this why our brains are so special and why we feel this connection to something greater than ourselves. There really could be a big "universal brain" out there that connects us! From this point on in my book and theory, *I will refer to God as the "universal brain" for this very reason.*

> ***Then God said, "Let us make man in our image, after our likeness. And let them have dominion over the fish of the sea and over the birds of the heavens and over the livestock and over all the earth and over every creeping thing that creeps on earth." (Genesis 1:26, English Standard Version)***

I recently found an article published in the *Huffington Post UK* on 11-27-2012 written by Michael Rundle. http://www.huffingtonpost.co.uk/2012/11/27/physicists-universe-giant-brain_n_2196346.html I've decided to include the article below; I believe science is on the right track with this idea.

PHYSICISTS FIND EVIDENCE THAT THE UNIVERSE IS A "GIANT BRAIN"

The idea of the universe as a "giant brain" has been proposed by scientists—and science fiction writers—for decades.

But now physicists say there may be some evidence that it's actually true, in a sense.

According to a study published in *Nature's Scientific Reports*, the universe may be growing in the same way as a giant brain—with the electrical firing between brain cells "mirrored" by the shape of expanding galaxies.

The results of a computer simulation suggest that "natural growth dynamics"—the way that systems evolve—are the same for different kinds of networks—whether it's the Internet, the human brain or the universe as a whole.

A coauthor of the study, Dmitri Krioukov from the University of California San Diego, said that while such systems appear very different, they have evolved in very similar ways. The result, they argue, is that the universe really does grow like a brain. The study raises profound questions about how the universe works, Krioukov said.

"For a physicist it's an immediate signal that there is some missing understanding of how nature works," he told Space.com.

The team's simulation modeled the very early life of the universe, shortly after the big bang, by looking at how quantum units of spacetime smaller than subatomic particles 'networked' with each other as the universe grew.

They found that the simulation mirrored that of other networks. Some links between similar nodes resulted in limited growth, while others acted as junctions for many different connections.

For instance, some connections are limited and similar—like a person who likes sports visiting many other sports websites—and some are major and connect to many other parts of the network, like Google and Yahoo.

No, it doesn't quite mean that the universe is "thinking"—but as has been previously pointed out online, it might just mean there's more similarity between the very small and the very large than first appearances suggest.

Now that you've read the article, what do you think about it?

Does the existence of God or the "universal brain" sound crazy now? Maybe God or the "universal brain" can really see what we do at all time, especially if our own brains have some constant cosmic connection to the big "universal brain." Maybe he can see through our own eyes! The whole concept of God does not sound so crazy when you think scientifically!

If there is a God or "universal brain" out there that can connect with our own physical/biological brains, how crazy does prayer sound now? Maybe that is the reason why so many people BELIEVE that prayer works—perhaps it really does!

If there is a God or "universal brain" out there, how crazy does it sound to use your brain and spirit to connect with it? That's why I think the key to our universe is in our own bodies, not out in space! I think we could use our spirits and consciousness to connect with the universe and travel space. Do I sound crazy, or do I sound realistic? Do these ideas seem plausible?

I now want to start describing how I visually imagine the universe. I know we think we have a picture of how our universe looks, but how do we know we are accurate and correct when we measured and created the maps of the universe? The diagram below illustrates how I picture the universe. Remember we once made maps of the earth we thought were accurate, and they were flat.

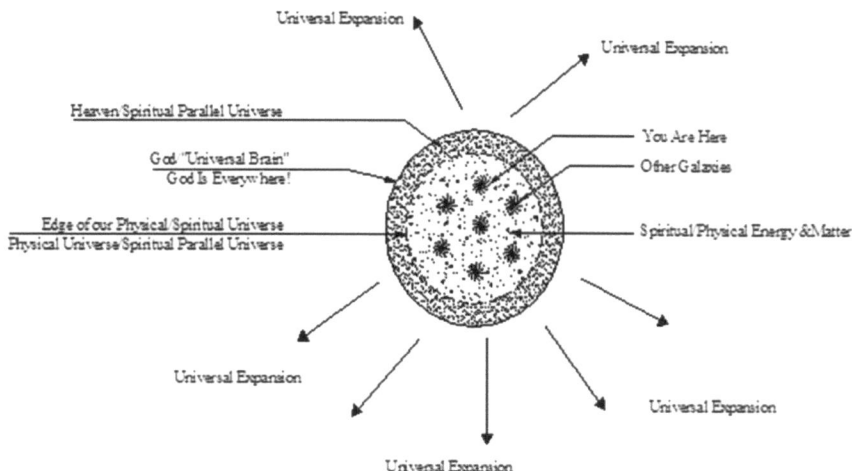

This is how I imagine the universe in my mind. Granted, the shape could be different, but this is the basic concept.

The definition of a membrane—a thin, flexible layer of tissue that covers, lines, separates, or connects cells or parts of an organism.

That definition is interesting to me, because membranes can both separate and connect cells and parts of organisms. If God is a "universal brain" that is biological and alive, and he is the membrane that separates our physical universe from our spiritual universe, it would seem possible according to that definition. The spiritual realm could pass back and forth through this membrane while still separating the spiritual universe from the physical/biological universe. If spirits have zero dimension and zero mass, they could pass back and forth through the membrane that keeps physical objects like human bodies (physical mass) out! This seems both plausible and logical.

Notice that my image of the universe also resembles a biological cell!

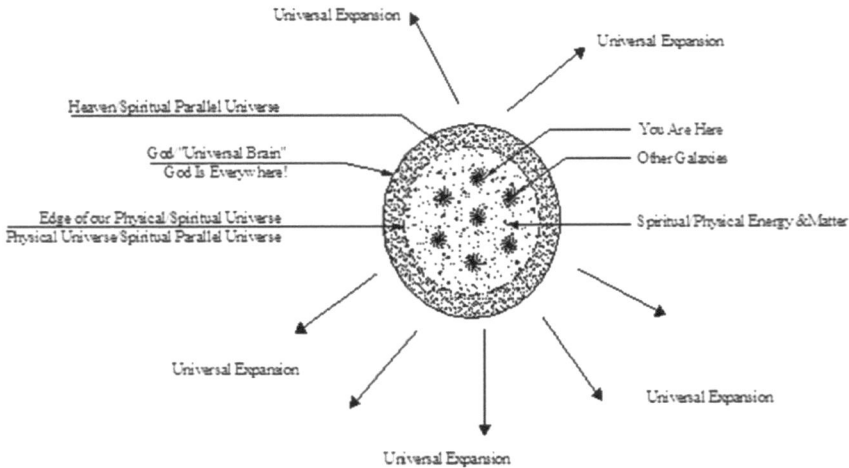

If the universe is biological and alive, is it really crazy to think about it like a cell? Cells do make up life! We are created from single cells, so why couldn't the universe be one big living cell? Membranes are used to both connect and separate, so why couldn't this "universal brain" do both? Separate us from God physically and biologically, while still keeping us connected spiritually. If God is just one big "universal brain" that is biological/spiritual, why couldn't he create our physical/biological bodies and also our spiritual bodies to keep us connected with our creator? If God is a "universal brain," it explains why we feel that our brains are the keys to our identities. Does the idea of God seem crazy now? Or is it starting to sound logical?

Last night when I was relaxing, I found myself on Facebook. I was just sort of surfing when I came across someone's post, and it struck me that this post was similar to the point I was trying to make in my dimensions chapter. I do not know who wrote this, **and I will not take the credit.** This post makes exactly the point I am trying to make here. I will let you read it for yourself and let you form your own opinion. This is a conversation between two identical twins in their mother's womb.

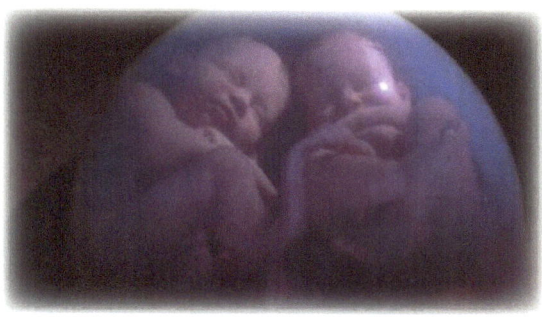

In the mother's womb were two babies. One asked the other: "Do you believe in life after delivery?" The other replied, "Why, of course; there has to be something after delivery. Maybe we are here to prepare ourselves for what will be later."

"Nonsense," said the first baby. "There is no life after delivery. What would that life be?"

"I don't know, but maybe it will be lighter than here. Maybe we will walk with our legs and eat with our mouths."

The first baby replied again, "That is absurd. Walking is impossible and eating with our mouths? That is ridiculous; we have umbilical cords that supply us with our nutrition. Life after delivery is impossible; the umbilical cord is too short for us to survive out there."

"Well, I think there IS something out there, and maybe it is different from here. Maybe we don't need our umbilical cord to survive out there," responded the second baby.

The first baby laughed at this and replied, "No one has ever come back from there. Delivery is the end of life, and after delivery there is nothing. You don't come back."

"Well, what about mother?" said the second baby. "Certainly she will take care of us when we are delivered."

IT'S ALL RELATIVE... THE GOD FACTOR...

The first baby laughed again. "Mother, you believe there's a mother out there? Where is this mother now? I do not see her. How can she exist if I have never seen her?"

The second baby said, "She is all around us. It is inside her that we live; without her we would not have this world. Sometimes when we are silent, I can hear her. I can perceive and feel her. I BELIEVE there is a life after delivery, and we are here to prepare ourselves for that reality".

That was the story I read. Now I want to remind you of how I imagine our universe and also how I imagine dimensions and dimension levels. Refer to the examples on the next page.

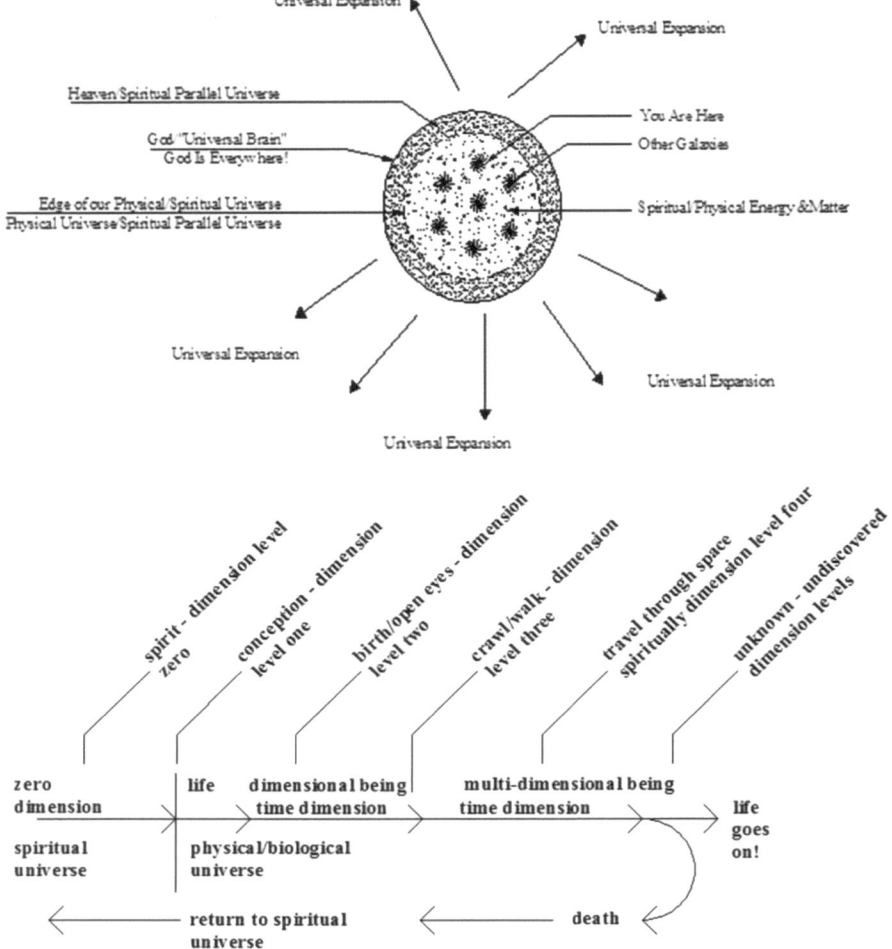

So, keep the story of the twins in mind when you think about possibilities. Could it be possible to have a heavenly father that we live in and grow in spiritually? Could this be similar to the process of birth, like we do when we are born physically from our own mothers? The earth is like one big womb; it holds us, surrounds us, and protects us. All religions are based on one simple idea: a higher being or God. Remember, God has many names.

> *For the scripture says, "Everyone who believes in him will not be put to shame." For there is no distinction between Jew and Greek; for the same Lord is Lord of all, bestowing all his riches on all who call on him. For, "Everyone who calls on the name of the Lord will be saved." (Romans 10:11–13, English Standard Version)*

To me this sounds like a God who does not judge who you are as long as you submit and believe in a higher God or "universal brain." If we were born once physically, why is it so implausible to imagine we can be born again, spiritually, after physical death, as long as you believe in God, the "universal brain"? To me, it seems pretty obvious when you just sit back and examine everything **we think** we know as a species.

> *"And you will know the truth, and the truth will set you free." (John 8:32, English Standard Version)*

If we really do have a "universal brain" or God out there, then these passages from the Bible would make sense:

> *Do not be conformed to this world, but be transformed by the renewal of your mind, that by testing you discern what is the will of God, what is good, acceptable, and perfect. (Romans 12:2, English Standard Version)*

> *You keep him in perfect peace whose mind is stayed on you, because he trusts in you. (Isaiah 26:3, English Standard Version)*

> **He is a double-minded man, unstable in all his ways. (James 1:8, English Standard Version)**

Think about that last passage. It sounds to me like they were describing humankind. If we have both a physical/biological brain and a spiritual consciousness that goes with it, you would have a double-minded man (human beings).

> **And whatever you ask in prayer, you will receive, if you have faith. (Matthew 21:22 English Standard Version)**

If God is a "universal brain," why couldn't we connect in prayer with our physical/biological brains? If a biological/spiritual God or "universal brain" created us then this next passage from the Bible would also make sense:

> **If then you have been raised with Christ, seek the things that are above, where Christ is, seated at the right hand of God. Set you minds on things that are above, not on things that are on earth. (Colossians 3:1–2, English Standard Version)**

Remember that science came up with the concept of the "universal brain;" I am just pointing out the similarities I see between that theory and God himself. Jesus said that God lives in you. Is our brain our connection with God? Does our (physical/biological) brain connect us to the universal (spiritual/biological) brain, or God? I would like to think so! Jesus says God lives in us, so let's use our brains!

Let's say that God/ the "universal brain" could be out there somewhere and we could cosmically connect with him. Meditation and physic abilities sure seem like a good place to start looking for answers. How else could you connect to that cosmic "universal brain" with our own physical/spiritual/biological brain? How else could you connect something physical with something that is an entity, except through prayer, meditation, and a psychic connection? But if God is the universe, which acts as a universal brain, maybe we could connect our physical brains also.

My Theory (Part B) Is God A Universal Brain?

The problem with scientists is that they want to see this God/the "universal brain" with their physical eyes before they will believe it. God is not physical. Physical things die, and God cannot die! Maybe that's why the universe is infinite. There are physical things we cannot see with our naked eye; why can't there be spiritual things that we can't see with the naked (physical) eye? I do believe in a "universal brain;" I call him God!

If scientists can imagine invisible parallel universes, why can't they imagine a spiritual universe and call it heaven? Some scientists think there may be several parallel universes out there. I believe there is only one, **and I do call it heaven!** If they can imagine an invisible universe, why can't they imagine an invisible God? They say they don't have evidence. The evidence is everywhere, but you have to believe in God in the first place! ***It's all relative to the observer!***

Scientific theories talk about invisible parallel universes and dimensions and about a "universal brain." They are describing souls, heaven, and God. Souls are an invisible (zero-dimensional) entity; heaven is an invisible parallel universe; and God is an invisible "universal brain"! Why do people not see this, or am I just a lunatic? Scientists can't see it because they don't believe in it!

That's why Jesus told us to believe. He said everything he could without giving away the whole secret!

Science wants to see the evidence, but remember what people who have had near-death experiences have told us. They say living beings are not allowed to see the face of God. We can only see God with our spiritual selves. Scientists will never be allowed to see God physically with their eyes, but I believe that if THEY believe in him, they will find him for us and advance us to the next level of the human race!

Now if membranes are biological tissue that can connect parts of an organism, isn't it possible that God is such a membrane? Isn't it possible that we live in God, and he lives in us, in our brains and souls? If membranes are part of an organism, organisms are biological and alive, and that means God lives! Why can't he be a spiritual/biological organism? He does not have to be physical and have a physical body.

After all this, having a real soul and connecting to a real God sure seem possible to me! When you try to put it scientifically, God, the "universal brain," created another person, just like us (someone with a brain), in order to tell us the truth about the universe. Does that seem crazy? Jesus Christ was a real person. If God is our father, why wouldn't he just tell us the truth about the universe? Do you lie to your kids about life? No, you tell them the truth: the good and the bad.

Think about Occam's razor—the principal that in explaining a thing, no more assumptions should be made than are necessary.

> ***And you will know the truth, and the truth will set you free. (John 8:32, English Standard Version)***

God is supposed to be our creator, our parent; you have to think of him like that and then relate the idea to your soul. Your physical mother gave you your life and a physical body; your spiritual father gave you a soul or spiritual body. Why does Jesus sound so crazy? If you had a child, you would try to show him or her answers without giving it away. You want to teach children so they learn and grow. Well, so does God, our "universal brain." So really, if God or the "universal brain" is out there and wants to communicate with us, why not send down another person just like us, with a brain perfectly in tune to the "universal brain," just to tell us the truth? **Jesus Christ!**

Why does there have to be so much mystery? You wouldn't make life hard like that on your child. Why can't life be this simple? Jesus says "I am the way, the truth, and the life:" he is simple and truthful.

Remember, Jesus was a real person; other people didn't just make him up. Science knows he was a real person, and real people witnessed his death; they also can't find his body to this day, because of the resurrection! Why can we find dinosaur bones and not his body? Remember, before you start to close your mind, time does not exist to God! Time is physical, and God is not. Time cannot exist to a "universal brain" that is an entity and everywhere. Jesus and the dinosaurs both existed. I do know, however, when I saw the Shroud of Turin, that I was looking at Jesus.

Now, do the ideas of heaven and souls, life after death, and God as a "universal brain" sound crazy? Do near-death experiences and people claiming to have seen God sound so crazy now? How about using your brain and spirit to travel through space and other dimension levels?

In the following chapters, I will discuss a few other scientific theories, including string and superstring theory; black holes and whites holes; matter and antimatter; and dark matter and dark energy. I will take these modern scientific theories and tie them into my own theory using God as the "universal brain" factor.

I will first explore string theory and superstring theory.

STRING THEORY

String theory is a theory used by quantum physicists rather than astrophysicists, and when explained simply, it is actually very easy to understand. I will explain it the same way I learned it, and I learned it by keeping it simple.

In this next example, there are two posts connected by a cable suspended between them.

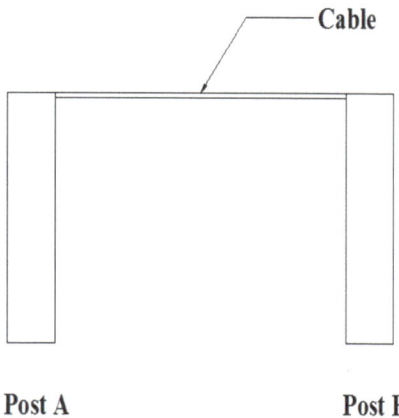

From a distance, the cable will look like a flat line without dimension, running from point A to point B. Now if you were to shrink yourself down to the size of an ant, you would be able to run along this cable, and if this cable were hollow and had an opening, you would be able to enter the cable. This is the basic concept of string theory: The part of the concept is that we are too big to see the dimensions or enter them, or even realize they exist for that matter.

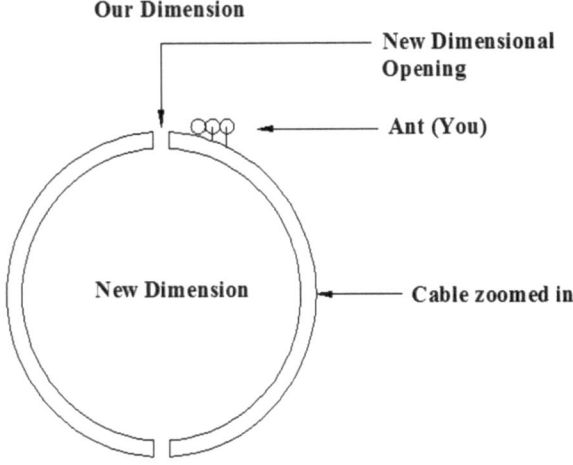

That's string theory on a very basic level. It definitely makes me think. I will tie it into my theory in just a little bit, but I wanted to explain the concept first.

SUPERSTRING THEORY

Superstring theory is based on string theory. I personally believe superstring theory is part of the key to the universe. I think the concept of string theory combined with superstring theory ***is a step toward understanding how life is created***. Keep that in mind as you follow my thought, because it continues through the section of the book that discusses black and white holes section, as well as the section that addresses different types of matter. But I do think these theories are part of the creation of life!

Superstring theory has basically the same concept of dimensions as string theory, but on a particle level. We are talking single protons, neutrons, and electrons. The theory goes like this: physicists have found this energy, like an electric spark, inside these particles that can vibrate! Scientists believe, and I agree, that these vibrating particles could be the key to traveling to different dimensions or, in my case, dimension levels. I just think it could work differently than science's explanation.

Physicists believe this energy spark can vibrate at different variations or patterns, and when they do, the spark produces and expels the different types of particles that make up the physical world around us. Physicists believe these different vibration patterns release other particles like protons, neutrons, and electrons, depending on the frequency or vibration pattern! These different particles bond together and eventually make up the physical world around us.

The problem or catch with superstring theory is that it **mathematically** does NOT work with a universe with ONLY three dimensions of space. It only works with ten dimensions of space and one dimension of time! That means this theory only works if there are other dimension levels out there. If you consider my example of dimension levels, we should still have seven other dimension levels we could achieve!

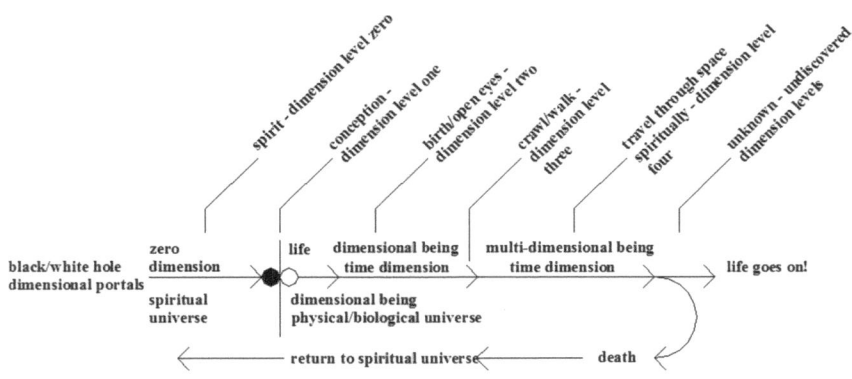

I think those other seven undiscovered dimension levels could be the key to our growth as a human species, before we truly understand how the universe works. I think our next step in the dimension level chain is figuring out how to travel through space. To do that using our spirit and our physical bodies, we would go from being simply dimensional beings to multidimensional beings. In this way, it would be possible to be in two places at once: your physical body still alive on earth while your spirit or consciousness traveled through space. I think that is the next step for us as humans.

Science looks at superstring theory this way (I hope I get this right since I am no quantum physicist): they take two particles and smash them together at nearly the speed of light, and they hope those two electric sparks will create a lot of energy. They are trying to send some of that energy to another dimension. That is what the particle accelerator does in Switzerland.

When physicists talk about string and superstring theory, they describe what they have discovered mathematically as twenty special numbers. They believe those twenty special numbers could possibly describe those other missing dimensions. I do not believe that they have published much about these numbers; I don't know what the numbers are. I should say that mathematics has never been my strength; I was always into science and biology. I will try to explain this with the limited amount of information I have. If you would like to learn more you can research octonions.

As children, we all learn about numbers. We start with counting, followed by addition, subtraction, multiplication, and division. But mathematicians know that the number system we study in school is but one of many possibilities. Other kinds of numbers are important for understanding geometry and physics. Among the strangest alternatives are *octonions*. Largely neglected since their discovery in 1843, in the past few decades they have assumed a curious importance in string theory. And indeed, if string theory is a correct representation of the universe, they may explain why the universe has the number of dimensions it does.

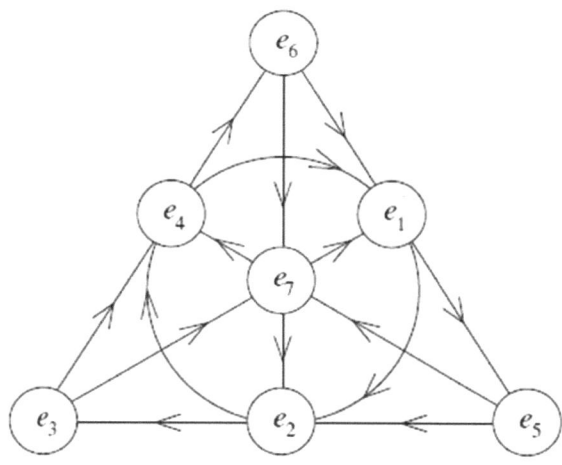

The Octonions

This is the octonions formula. This is the best I can do for you math types; don't ask me to figure it out, though. I am not bringing them up to try to figure out what they mean; I am just trying to explain how they fit into string theory.

Physicists describe these twenty numbers like a dial on a control panel for the universe. If someone was to come up and change even one setting on these controls, the universe would never exist—it is that balanced and connected. How could randomness in nature create something so intricate and balanced? I believe everything was perfectly created and balanced, like it was planned. What's the more logical solution: that all this perfect balance of creation was made from randomness in the universe, or that God/ the "universal brain" created such balance?

Physicists also believe these ten dimensions are all interconnected! Think of the dimension levels again and how, as we grow up, we progress through them naturally. Perhaps as a human species, we travel up these dimension levels as we grow, slowly moving up the dimension level chain. Maybe our next jump is to become multidimensional rather than simply dimensional beings, remember right now you can only occupy one point in the universe at a time (dimensional). If you were to leave your body on earth and travel through space using your consciousness, you would be in two points in space at one time (multidimensional).

Here are my thoughts on string theory and superstring theory. Could you make your brain particles (neurons or particles in your neurons) vibrate through deep meditation or intense concentration, and super-charge the brain, causing those particles to vibrate at a special cosmic frequency? Could you find a small dimension like the one described in string theory inside of our bodies, or could you create one? What if the dimensions are not physical themselves but spiritual? How could we ever find them then unless we looked inside our spirits? Our souls are the only thing spiritual we have in this physical universe. Could you create that spiritual dimension by making your brain particles vibrate as described in superstring theory, and then create a small spiritual-dimensional opening like in string theory? Who knows, but I like to think it could be possible!

THE PARTICLE ACCELERATOR

The particle accelerator in Switzerland is a pretty cool machine. For those of you who have never heard of it, I will explain it. It is a very large machine that looks like a big doughnut with a hole cut out of the center. In this machine, scientists take hydrogen protons and send them around in a circle, trying to reach the speed of light. Then they take either hydrogen electrons or other hydrogen protons and send them into the machine in the opposite direction, trying to reach the speed of light. Then physicists hope the particles collide and smash into each other.

This is a simple example of how the particle accelerator works. When scientists first started smashing protons together, they didn't know what was going to happen. They even theorized that it might produce a black hole. They have not produced a black hole, nor have they been successfully able to send the energy from smashed particles to a different dimension.

I am now going to explain to you how I see the particle accelerator fitting into my theory. I will also try to incorporate both string and superstring theory into my theory. You will have to keep your mind open and imagine a little bit here.

I want to start out by saying why I think scientists are having a problem with their particle accelerator. I don't actually experiment with the machine, so I don't know for a fact—these are just ideas of mine. The reason I think they are having problems with their experiments is Einstein's theory of relativity. If we are going to send something into space at light speed, doesn't the object have to be motionless? Here is where I see the problem (in my head anyway): both the particle and the targeted dimensions are in motion. If I look at that particle from outside the solar system, it is still moving through the universe at sixty-seven thousand miles per hour.

I think the second reason they are having trouble is that they are still thinking ONLY physically. They don't account for the biological/

spiritual aspects of the universe. It is difficult to hit a moving target. Physical dimensions move while spiritual (nonphysical) dimensions do not. There is no mass for gravity to interfere with! You need a spiritual (zero mass) particle and target, not a physical particle and target.

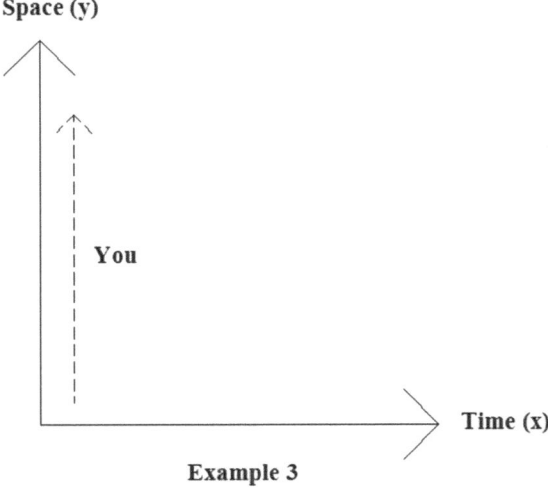

Example 3

This is what we are trying to accomplish (basically) with the particle accelerator, but we are using particles instead of living human beings.

But, this is how I see the particle science is using now in their machine.

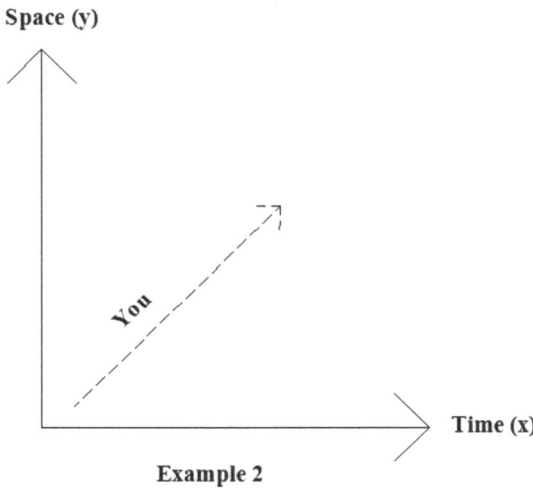

Example 2

The Particle Accelerator

The particle is still moving if you observe it from outside the solar system, and the particle, the machine, and earth are all moving at sixty-seven thousand miles per hour. It's all relative to how you observe your particle. So, if you are using a physical particle on earth and targeting another physical dimension (whether larger or small), they are both still in motion. Because they are both physical things, they will stay in motion and subjected to the effect of gravity. That's my problem with the particle accelerator; it's all relative to how you observe the particle.

An object at rest will remain at rest unless acted on by an unbalanced force. An object in motion continues in motion with the same speed and in the same direction unless acted upon by an unbalanced force. This is Newton's law of inertia.

I have one more problem with the particle accelerator. They are trying to send something to another dimension. I think at the particle level, the process might be reversed, in that things travel to us from other dimensions at that level (this idea is based on my understanding of string and superstring theory). The particles might also need to have zero mass, maybe that's the problem? I will explain more when I get to black holes and white holes; I just want you to remember that I mentioned it; because I will come back to it.

Back to the first problem, though, and why I don't think we are observing the particles correctly. I have many different ideas that I will throw out there, but they are all based on one concept: I think **particles come from** other dimensions, and I will explain why if you can just follow my thought process.

Let's look at how we are observing the particle. We are viewing it as an outside observer, from a distance. Think about Einstein's theory, and this time we will use another example to show how observation makes the difference. We are going to use a baseball example.

Let's imagine we have a flatbed truck traveling down the road at fifty miles per hour and we have a pitcher (P) and a catcher (C) on the truck. We also have a person with a radar gun standing on the truck with the baseball players, ready to track the speed of the ball.

It's All Relative... The God Factor...

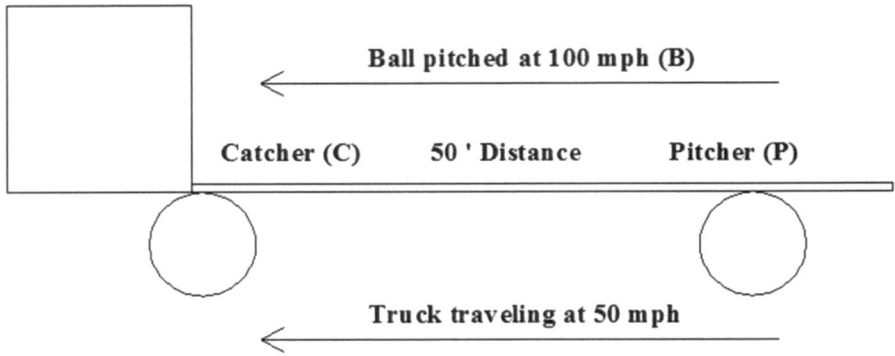

If you were that person standing on the truck and you tracked that pitch with your radar gun, it would still register one hundred miles per hour even though the truck is also traveling at fifty miles per hour. If you then did the same experiment but you got off the truck and stood on the side of the road with your radar gun, the pitch would read one hundred and fifty miles per hour. That additional fifty miles per hour is a variable that changes **RELATIVE TO WHERE YOU ARE AS THE OBSERVER.**

So take that same concept and apply it to that physical particle inside the particle accelerator. Depending on where you observe it determines whether it's truly motionless or not. Returning to the problem with our particle accelerator, we are not observing the particle close enough.

Now let's look at the experiment in reverse, we are reversing which direction the ball is being pitched but the truck is still travelling in the same direction. The particle can be the ball and the universe can be the truck. I never did see the experiment done in reverse; I just learned about this concept through the first example of the truck, the one I just shared with you. I am going to go with what common sense tells me. I could be wrong, but this is how my brain works, and since I don't have the resources to perform this experiment myself, I am just going to apply common sense.

The Particle Accelerator

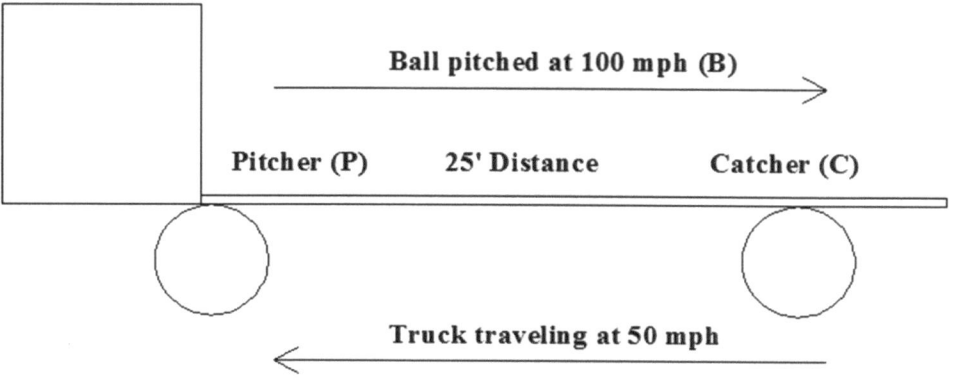

Now if we did the same experiment, first on the truck and then from the side of the street, what results would we get? I am assuming (based on common sense) that if I did the first experiment from the truck, I would get a radar speed of one hundred miles per hour; but because the target is moving toward the ball this time, the actual distance traveled would contract to twenty-five feet. Then if we did it from the street and checked the radar, we would only read fifty miles per hour, because the truck's speed would cancel out the other fifty miles per hour. So as we've learned from Einstein, it's all relative to the observer. The only consistent reading we got was when we got as close as possible to that ball to cancel out the motion of the truck. Now think of it this way: the earth and our solar system is the truck, and both our pitcher and catcher (particle and target) are moving.

So I think first, we need to observe our particle as close as possible. Then, how do we become motionless in the universe? That question brings me to this question: where is the absolute center of the universe? To answer that question, I look to science and astrophysics. The cosmological principal answers that very question.

The cosmological principal: The center of the universe is everywhere. No matter where you are in the universe, everything else is expanding out at the same rate. So, scientifically speaking, you are the center of your universe.

I bring up the cosmological principal because if we are living in a three-dimensional universe with volume, and that volume is in motion, where is the only still point in the universe? It would be at the absolute center. According to science, the absolute center of the universe is inside of me. If I am the center of my universe, how do I get to the true absolute center of myself without looking inside myself? The answer is you can't. In order to become motionless in this universe, we have to look inside ourselves. How do we find a motionless particle? We need to find the particles inside ourselves instead of looking at external particles, such as a hydrogen proton. The only way to find a motionless particle from within is to look to the brain, spirit, or consciousness. You can make your mind motionless!

That is the problem with the particle accelerator. The physical particle has mass, which we know gravity affects. The problem with physical particles is that when they near the speed of light, the mass of the particle itself expands and slows down. A particle without physical mass or a spiritual (zero mass) particle might do the trick!

The second problem is the target destination. If it's a physical dimension whether big or small, it is in motion, and it is easy to miss moving targets. We need a motionless target or motionless dimension. We should aim to send energy to a nonphysical, spiritual dimension like heaven. We need a dimension that has no motion and no physical dimension. Why can't we consider heaven to be the target dimension? Because people don't believe it exists? It doesn't have to be heaven; it could be a nonphysical (spiritual) dimension in this universe. Why couldn't that be out there? But if it is out there and it is nonphysical, why would we think our physical bodies would be allowed to travel there? Why wouldn't we also assume we would need something nonphysical (spiritual) to send?

This is my idea, if we can make our brains motionless, why couldn't we hook ourselves up to the particle accelerator and try to send our consciousness through it at light speed?

If you can make your mind and consciousness still through meditation, why couldn't you travel to a spiritual dimension? We already have the technology to try something like this. We have the particle accelerator, and we have the technology to communicate with computers using only our thoughts and brain. If we can communicate with a computer using only our thoughts, why can't we send the computer a consciousness? Send it out at the speed of light and back before our brains could even physically register it was gone? Your brain can only process things so fast. What if you could send out neurons with your DNA and consciousness at light speed, before the physical part of your mind knew they were gone? Can we make our neurons travel at the speed of light in our own minds through the power of meditation and supercharge our brains? I think the brain is powerful enough to do it if we could figure out how to control that power, but maybe using the particle accelerator could be the key…who knows?

I do think that hooking up to a computer and being able to communicate with it could be the first step. Then if you were to meditate and make your brain and consciousness still and enter the computer, could you then send yourself into the particle accelerator? I believe it's possible to teleport with your mind, sending your consciousness out at the speed of light while keeping your physical body here. If your physical body and brain remained here on Earth but your spirit and consciousness were out traveling at the speed of light to other dimensions, you would truly be multidimensional.

If we could send our thoughts out at the speed of light, faster than our brains can process them, would that stimulate an out-of-body experience? Could that help us to learn to control our consciousness and create out-of-body experiences at will? If we could do that, we could use our consciousness to explore space whenever we wanted. If we used our souls or consciousness, we would have no physical mass, and gravity would have no effect on us. Without the encumbrance of a physical body, perhaps we could beam our consciousness through space like a laser. There are lots of possibilities once you open your mind to this idea. First, you have to believe that you have a soul; if you believe you have a soul, you must believe it goes somewhere when you die.

I think we have built the first step in a teleportation device, the particle accelerator; I just don't think we are using it quite right. Perhaps the direction of your thoughts within the particle accelerator matters; maybe the motion of the universe has some effect on the particles we are using now, especially physical ones that have mass, which gravity can affect.

In order to test this theory, someone would have to volunteer to go into the particle accelerator. This would require much caution and care. I am aware of what could happen physically to people who might try this, but I want to talk about one man who had an accident with a particle accelerator. I've included the article below that I found online to illustrate this point.

Neuroscience Cases: The Man Who Put His Head in a Particle Accelerator

"Have you been injured at work in an accident that wasn't your fault?" The terrible advertisements for companies like lawyers4u typically refer to fairly mundane work injuries, such as falling off of ladders or slipping on a wet floor. One man's work-related accident was a great deal more spectacular. Anatoli Petrovich Bugorski accidentally put his head in a particle accelerator.

To this day, he remains the only living person to have done so and survived. But, how does one go about accidentally putting one's head into a particle accelerator? Well, on July 13, 1978, Bugorski was working on the U-70 synchrotron at the Institute for High Energy Physics in Protvino, Russia. A small piece of equipment was malfunctioning and in the process of fixing it, he leaned in too far and came into contact with the proton beam. When later asked to describe what it was like, he said he saw a flash of light that was "brighter than a thousand suns." But, amazingly, he felt no pain.

Very quickly after the incident had occurred, the left side of his face swelled beyond all recognition. The beam entered his skull at the back of his head, with the exit wound close to his nose. After a few days the skin at the entry and exit points peeled away showing the path the beam took through the skin, skull, and brain. His prognosis was extremely poor; he was taken to a clinic in Moscow where they expected to observe him die over a period of two to three weeks.

The proton beam was about 200,000 rads. Previous data indicated that 1000 rads would be enough to kill a human (even the famously radioactively robust cockroach will die after 20,000). However, the specific effects of a proton beam traveling at the speed of light were not known.

After the initial incident, the path of the beam began to burn through his brain. This continued for two years until the left side of his face was completely paralyzed. Apparently, this has had an almost Botox-like effect on his face. The left side of his face has been described as being "frozen in time," whilst the right side of his face has aged normally. Other than this, Anatoli has had surprisingly few neurological symptoms. Over the initial twelve years after the incident, he had occasional petit mal seizures. More recently, he has had an increased number of grand mal seizures.

Anatoli continued his life after it became apparent he was not at risk of immediate death. He completed his PhD and worked as a researcher for many years (Google Scholar lists some of his research). Not long ago, he decided to make himself available to Western researchers, but he did not have the money to relocate from Protvino. He thinks he would make a brilliant research subject: "This is, in effect, an unintended test of proton warfare," he claims. More to the point, he believes, "I am being tested. The human capacity for survival is being tested."

That was an article posted online, *"physics |B Good Science Blog,"* posted March 28, 2011 http://bgoodscience.wordpress.com/tag/physics-2/

The fact that he survived is not only a good sign, but it's a sign that it's physically possible to interact with a particle accelerator, which means that it could be a valuable tool for human space travel. Now that I've shared some of my thoughts about the particle accelerator and its place in my theory, I am going to discuss opposites in nature and how I think that they are another key to figuring out how our universe works. I will also return to the second reason I think scientists are looking at superstring theory backward. You will see where I am going with all of this as I start talking about opposites.

NATURE AND THE LANGUAGE OF OPPOSITES

Before I continue on, I need to talk about opposites found in nature. This will lead us to the rest of my theory and will allow me to tie my ideas together.

I want to start this section by reminding everyone of one of our most basic laws of physics: every action has an equal and opposite reaction. I know everyone reading this book has noticed some of the opposites in nature; I am going to start out with the most obvious and work toward those that are less obvious.

Let's start with light and dark (night and day); black and white; and good and evil. If we are going to believe that there is a God or "universal brain" out there that is good, then we must also believe the opposite (evil) is also out there. If we believe in the possibility of God or a "universal brain," which is a good entity, we must also believe that an evil entity and an evil energy are out there as well.

If there is a good entity in this physical world, there must be an evil entity also. Not only does the Bible say he exists, but our law of physics also says he must exist; that means that *Satan and evil can be real!* Why do people believe in a good entity but not an evil one? We choose to see what we want to see.

If there can be both physical and spiritual goodness like love, then physical and spiritual evil also exists. Don't tell me that love is not a real thing. Until someone can prove to me love is not real, I will continue to believe evil is also real. In the physical world, we encounter positives and negatives everywhere. Good and evil are nothing more than positive and negative entities. Good and evil are spiritual forms of the positives and negatives we find in the material world.

As I start to point out more of these opposites, keep in mind that if they can exist physically, there's no reason why they can't exist spiritually as well. I am going to start small and work my way toward some of the big opposites in our physical universe.

The first and most obvious opposites are physical particles themselves. We have protons, neutrons, and electrons, which make up atoms and all forms of physical matter. These are positively and negatively charged particles. If you think of them with a spiritual aspect, they are positive and negative energies in our physical world.

I am sure physicists and biologists can think of more opposites at this level; since I am neither, I can only think of the particles. But if physical matter exists at the level of the particle, why can't spiritual matter exist at that level as well? Why can't our physical, material world include parts of the spiritual world that we may be connected to?

How about the human sperm and egg—two OPPOSITE chromosomes used to create life? Two halves combine to make a whole being. That's why we need to look at the opposites in nature, to help us figure out the meaning of the universe. If we take all the opposites of the universe and start following their trail, we might discover how the opposites in nature combine to tell the story of the universe.

In nature, opposites attract; just look at magnets. Human chromosomes need two opposites to make a whole. I think that's part of the key to unlocking life's mysteries and the creation of life. Besides magnets and chromosomes attracting, protons, neutrons, and electrons all attract to form atoms, which are the building blocks of all physical matter. The atom consists of opposites attracting and bonding to form one new creation. When you look at opposites and talk about attraction, you must then talk about things that naturally repel each other. Two similar magnets repel naturally and will not bond to each other, but you can't create a new human with two male chromosomes, you need an opposite for the creation of life.

What about dimensions? If we have physical dimensions and we know they exist, why can't spiritual dimensions exist in opposition to physical dimensions? I want to point out that I think there is an opposite parallel (spiritual) universe. As I stated in previous chapters, I also believe that there are spiritual dimensions in this universe. *After all, if there are physical dimensions in this universe, why can't spiritual dimensions also exist in this universe?*

If physical beings exist, why can't spiritual beings exist? It takes two halves to make a whole being, just like two chromosomes. Perhaps we need both a physical body and a spiritual body to create a being. Does that really sound crazy? If souls can exist, and good and evil can exist, why can't angels and demons exist? Flip back to the optical illusions pictures in this book and tell me you still trust everything you see with your physical eyes!

If our physical universe exists, why can't an opposite parallel (spiritual) universe exist? This is the part of the spiritual realm I consider heaven. If everything else we have talked about can exist, why can't heaven exist? If God out there, where is that being's realm? To take things further, if heaven can exist, why can't hell exist? I think people want to deny these possibilities in order to excuse their often thoughtless behavior. I think people don't want to believe in God because they don't want to believe in hell or the possibility that their actions might have far-reaching, negative consequences. But if science thinks a "universal brain" exists–God, as I like to call him—then hell is a definite possibility. If God or a "universal brain" created us, why wouldn't he judge us and either reward or punish us? Every other parent in the world does. I think humanity needs to straighten up and open its eyes!

If there are physical particles invisible to the naked eye floating around this universe, why can't there by spiritual particles invisible to the naked eye floating around this universe as well? If those physical particles can create physical energy, why can't spiritual particles create spiritual energy? Just because we haven't found any spiritual particles yet does not mean they don't exist. Spiritual objects have no mass and are invisible to the naked eye! If we can move physically in a physical dimension, why couldn't we move spiritually in a spiritual dimension?

Now it's time to talk about some other opposites in space: black holes and white holes; and matter and antimatter.

BLACK HOLES AND WHITE HOLES

Black Holes

I bring up black and white holes right after my chapter on opposites for a big reason, and it's not just because one is black and one is white. I think we need to study these more, because I also think they could be a big key in how the universe works.

Let's start out by explaining how black holes work. Black holes are big, gravitational cosmic holes in space that are so strong that they can trap light (the one universal constant). The gravitational pull is so strong that it can actually warp space and time. Physicists theorize that if you were to enter a black hole, the force would be so strong that you would experience spaghettification. Basically, you would be stretched as thin as spaghetti and rip apart at the molecular level. It does not sound like we will be entering any black holes anytime soon, physically that is. Now that you know the basics of black holes, let's examine white holes, since they are a new idea, and no one has ever found one…yet!

White Holes

The concept of white holes is not very well known. Physicists theorize that when a black hole from this universe and another black hole from a **parallel universe** collide, the result is a white hole. *If science can believe that parallel universes are out there and they theorize about a "universal brain," why can't they just refer to them as God and heaven?*

I want to point out that they are saying something physical from this universe comes together with something from our opposite (I think spiritual) universe to create something whole, the white hole. This is the same comparison I made about needing both the physical body and the spiritual body to create life, also like how sperm and egg collide to create life!

It's interesting that scientists have named them "white holes." They sound similar to the tunnels of light people describe in near-death experiences. People often describe traveling to and from heaven in a tunnel of white light. People also claim to transform from physical beings to spiritual beings during these experiences—another example of opposites.

The next really interesting point about white holes is that *science theorizes* that they work the *opposite* way a black hole works! Instead of a strong gravitational energy sucking everything into it, the white hole spews out energy and particles. *Science also theorizes that if you entered a black hole, you might come out a white hole!* I agree with this idea to a certain extent, but I discuss it further later in the book.

I do agree with science that black holes and white holes could be possible dimension portals, but science looks at them as physical portals, whereas I look at them as spiritual portals for the creation and cycle of life. Don't forget that no one has actually found a white hole yet; it is just a theory like black holes once were. Einstein believed both were theoretically possible, and we have now found black holes!

Now, in order for black holes and white holes to work with my theory, you need to believe there is a God or "universal brain" out there and that there is also a parallel universe (heaven). That's why it's the God factor: it only works if you involve God. I also think that science is looking at black holes from the wrong point of view. Before I explain that opinion further, I want to discuss the search for actual white holes. Scientists and astrophysicists theorize that white holes are very unstable and don't last long, unlike black holes. If I were going to search for something in this universe, I would follow the path of opposites.

If black holes are big, black, stable, and out in space, I would start looking in the opposite direction for a white hole. I would start looking for something *small, white, instantaneous, and here on earth. This sounds like the spark of life that happens inside a woman's womb!*

I believe if scientists studied the moment of conception with a more religious and philosophical approach (not just a medical approach), they might find a tiny white hole on the quantum level! This connects to my idea, which I discussed in the chapter on string and superstring theory, that science had the direction backward. I think something is supposed to **come into our dimension at the quantum level**. I believe the physical body receives its spirit at the moment of conception! The two black holes, from two different universes, combine to create the white hole, which lets a spirit come through for the creation of life. That's how I think they work.

Science has been trying to push a particle through a one-way door; only spiritual matter can travel from the spiritual universe through the white hole to our physical universe. That one-way door is the white hole created at the quantum (particle) level inside a human womb! That's why I think we have never found one; we are looking in the wrong direction.

As I said, *I believe white holes are created on the quantum level at the moment of conception within a human womb!*

Think about this for a moment. If there is a God or "universal brain" and he did create black holes and white holes as dimensional portals between the two universes, why would he make an entry point as frightening as a black hole? If we were meant to enter it physically, as humans, why would he make the portal so brutal? It would kill us if we tried to enter a black hole physically. Why wouldn't he make a nice, white tunnel filled with light? Everything we have ever learned about death says we go into a white light.

I don't think we are meant to travel back up through the white hole to heaven except when we die. If we were able to travel through space, we would do so by using our spirit or consciousness to create an out-of-body experience. I imagine we might encounter those theoretical wormholes that scientists theorize about but cannot prove in that meditative state, a state where we encounter the world with our consciousness and not our physical eyes. I do believe wormholes exist but in the spiritual, zero-dimensional realm. We cannot see them with our physical, two-dimensional eyes.

I think the black holes and white holes are the big mixing bowl where science's primordial soup to life creates our spiritual body! I think the black and white holes give us our spirit and connect the spiritual body with the physical body in the creation of life.

I think that matter, both dark matter and antimatter, are mixed up in space and are then sucked through both of the black holes that collide and create the white hole. Then God or the "universal brain" gives us our spirit and consciousness, and we are conceived. We come out of a white hole, and then that miracle of life is created inside the womb. That's part of how I think black and white holes work. If I had to choose between entering a black hole and a white hole, I would choose, as a Christian, the white hole. God says he is the light. To reiterate, however, I think black and white holes are intended for the creation and cycle of life, not for traveling through space. That's what wormholes are for.

If a person happens to die or have a near-death experience, however, then I believe that person travels up the white hole back to heaven. ***Could you create a white hole inside your mind and enter it with your consciousness, creating a vision and experience of heaven and God?***

Now it's time to add matter and antimatter into the mix, but, again, they only fit into the theory if you add the God factor or the "universal brain" factor.

MATTER AND ANTIMATTER

Matter is the building block of all things physical, and it was created during the big bang. At the point of its creation, its opposite was also created—antimatter. Our entire physical universe is composed of matter. If our physical world consists of matter, why couldn't our spiritual world consist of antimatter? Antimatter exists in our universe. Scientists have recorded antimatter in our own atmosphere discharging off of lightning! Is it a coincidence that lightning is energy in the form of light, just like God, and it happens to discharge antimatter?

I am going to refer to antimatter as "spiritual" antimatter from now on, because I believe antimatter consists of the spiritual particles I referred to earlier, and that's how it fits into my theory (spiritually).

Science claims that "spiritual" antimatter vanished after the big bang, and only matter remained. If this were true, however, why can we still record it near lighting? How could it just vanish? Because scientists can't see it with the naked eye or explain it, they pretend it vanished. Did they ever think that it was spiritual matter, and that they could not see it because it is not a physical thing; that it never vanished at all?

A man by the name of Arthur Schuster (1851–1934) had a theory about antimatter that makes a lot of sense to me. His theory was that antimatter has the ***opposite effect*** with gravity; that physical mass has with gravity. This makes sense. If you have physical mass or matter, gravity can grab its physical form and affect it. If you happen to have the opposite charge as matter (antimatter) the effects would be the opposite.

Antimatter sounds like the perfect building block for a spiritual being. Could antimatter be inside of us? Perhaps our souls are composed of antimatter? God says a piece of him lives in us. Could antimatter be a connection to God?

It's All Relative... The God Factor...

The next really interesting part of Arthur Schuster's theory deals with the big bang. He thought that either during the big bang (or not long afterward), there were two separate masses of unstable matter and unstable antimatter that collided, and the two unstable masses bonded. He thought that when the two masses bonded and equalized, **they created two parallel universes** that separated and expanded apart.

That sounds a lot like how I imagine the universe. It's a little different, but it's still pretty close. I do believe we have two parallel universes: one physical/biological and one spiritual/biological. I think physical and spiritual matter make up our physical universe, and I think "spiritual" antimatter makes up our spiritual universe or heaven—the place God prepared for our souls!

> *And if I go and prepare a place for you, I will come back and take you to be with me that you may also be where I am. (John 14:3, New International Version)*

Often, when people describe heaven after near-death experiences, they describe it as here and now and everywhere. They describe it as all around us and earth-like, but still separate from the physical world. They also describe it as more real than this world!

I think heaven is made purely of "spiritual" antimatter while our physical realm also contains some antimatter along with the physical matter, and that's what gives us our souls and cosmic connection. Has anyone ever looked for antimatter in a human body?

It makes sense that our souls, if composed of "spiritual" antimatter, would connect us to our "universal brain" or God. Scientifically speaking, it sounds like God could exist! The idea definitely does not sound so crazy anymore—not to me, anyway.

> *Even though I walk through the valley of the shadow of death, I will fear no evil, for you are with me; your rod and your staff, they comfort me. You prepare a table before me in the presence of my enemies; you anoint my head with oil;*

my cup overflows. Surely your goodness and mercy shall follow me all the days of my life, and I shall dwell in the house of the Lord forever. (Psalm 23:4–6, English Standard Version)

And the dust returns to the earth as it was, and the spirit returns to the God who gave it. (Ecclesiastes 12:7, English Standard Version)

So this is just a quick recap of how I think everything I have talked about all fits. Your spirit from heaven enters a black hole, mixes with matter and "spiritual" antimatter, and comes out a white hole in the form of life. This occurs in the womb, at the moment of conception. Think about the dimension levels diagram again.

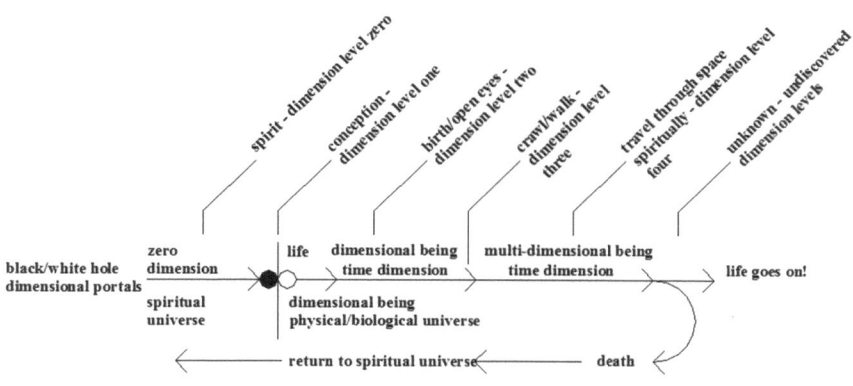

This is the same diagram, but this time I made a few changes and added some additional elements to help you visualize what I am thinking. I added the black and white holes into the picture along with the possibility for multidimensional space travel, by using both our souls and our physical consciousness through out-of-body experiences.

Below is an updated image of the universe.

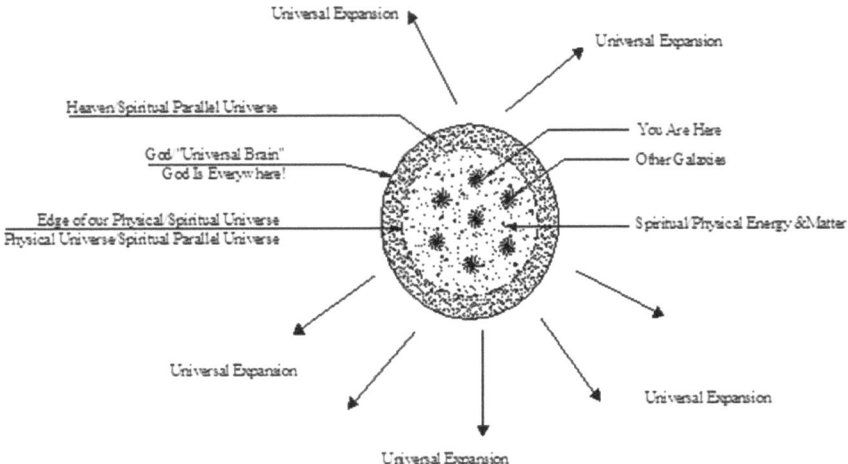

I think the black and white holes are the key that could bring astrophysics and quantum physics together, ultimately with life as the big picture. I do believe God is what brings it all together.

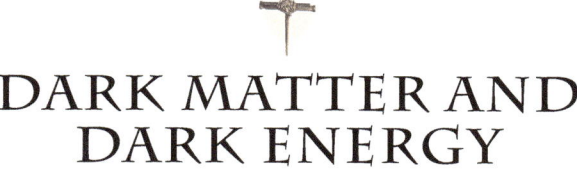

DARK MATTER AND DARK ENERGY

Dark matter and dark energy are also new discoveries, another variable we can add to the questions of the universe. Science believes that this dark matter and energy are heavy influences on our physical universe. I also believe this, and I have an idea about its capabilities and influence in our universe. It all fits right in with my theory.

Science estimates that the ratio of dark matter to physical, ordinary matter is actually 5:1 in our universe. This is how science estimates our universe: 5 percent is normal, physical matter, all the particles that make our physical universe; 25 percent is dark matter, and we don't know what this does; 70 percent is dark energy, and we also do not yet understand its role in our universe. Scientists leave out antimatter, which they believe has vanished. I believe that it still exists. I think the antimatter is spiritual matter.

Here is my attempt to add dark matter and dark energy into my theory, although you'll need a little spiritual imagination to make this work.

Our physical/biological universe consists of matter. Antimatter is possibly spiritual matter (what makes up heaven and God or the "universal brain"). Where is our opposite? If we have a "good" spiritual entity out there, where is the opposite "evil" entity? I think dark matter and dark energy are evil. In religious terms, they represent Satan.

One of the fascinating things science has said about antimatter is that when it comes into contact with matter, it *destroys it!* I know what everyone right now is thinking; if antimatter is heaven and God, our "universal brain," and it destroys matter that makes up our whole universe, including ourselves. Wouldn't God be destroying us on purpose? That contradicts everything! It doesn't if you look at it the way I see it; then it actually makes sense. You will have to follow along closely to understand my thought progression, because it's a big thought right here and will take a minute to explain.

Here we are as humans who are alive (physical/biological matter). I believe we are also spiritual beings, so we have to add "spiritual" antimatter into our composition. Even if we can't see it or have not discovered it inside of us yet, it does not it mean it can't exist. So we have the three universal aspects I believe we need to consider: physical, biological, and spiritual. I am going to refer to humans as the Physical Child or (PC) during this example.

If we have that "spiritual" parallel universe (heaven) made out of pure "spiritual" antimatter, we will also call God or the "universal brain" the "spiritual" antimatter. For the rest of this example, I am going to refer to God or the "universal brain" as "Heavenly Father" or (HF).

Now remember (PC) and (HF), because I will jump back to them. First, I have to finish explaining why I think dark matter and dark energy are Satan and his evil spiritual power. Then I will finish tying everything together.

Why is it dark? God is light, so its opposite or "enemy" would be darkness. Dark matter neither emits nor absorbs light! An article published on September 21, 2009 on physicsworld.com says that "new research on dark matter suggests it is made up of **dark protons** and **dark electrons** that are acted on by the **dark matter equivalent of the electromagnetic force.**" Wouldn't that be dark energy? Just because something is at the particle and mass level, <u>**why do we only consider its physical properties?**</u> Why can't that dark matter be biological and alive as well, or spiritual for that matter? This material seems like it could create an "evil" spiritual entity to me! I call that "evil" spiritual entity Satan! If God or the "universal brain" can exist, why can't Satan? People don't want to believe in Satan; it's inconvenient. If they don't believe in Satan, then they can't believe in God or that there may be long-lasting consequences to their actions.

Science also believes that dark matter particles are colliding with your atoms all the time inside your body. Thousands of dark matter particles enter your body every year and collide with your own atoms.

This is also why I believe that dark matter is Satan or "death." Are these collisions slowly breaking down the atoms in our bodies, causing aging and eventually death?

Think about these passages from the Bible:

> *In which you once walked, following the course of this world, following the prince of the power of the air, the spirit that is now at work in the sons of disobedience. (Ephesians 2:2, English Standard Version)*

> *And the great dragon was cast out, that old serpent, called the Devil, and Satan, which deceiveth the whole world: he was cast out into the earth, and his angels were cast out with him. (Revelations 12:9, King James Version, Cambridge Edition)*

Since we live in a universe that is biological and **ALIVE**, the opposite of life is death: Satan is death! The Bible says God is "***the way, the truth, and the life.***"

If Satan was banished from heaven to this universe, he would have become a physical entity, not a spiritual entity. He may be invisible, but he is still physical. All physical things that are biological in this universe can die, so Satan and death can be defeated. If Satan is nothing but "evil" matter, even dark matter, it is still matter; which means spiritual antimatter can destroy it. God can defeat Satan! If you don't think of dark matter as anything more than ordinary matter that is just "evil," then it's still just matter. I think "spiritual" antimatter could destroy both ordinary matter and "evil" matter/dark matter. Good defeats evil!

The Bible talks about spiritual warfare. Is there a battle going on in our universe between "evil" dark matter and "spiritual" antimatter?

> *For we do not wrestle against flesh and blood, but against the rulers, against the authorities, against the cosmic powers over this present darkness, against the spiritual forces of evil in the heavenly places. (Ephesians 6:12, English Standard Version)*

If we looked inside our own bodies at the particle level, would we discover dark matter inside of our own atoms? That would make sense if dark matter is Satan and death, and it would explain why we age and die. It would also explain how God destroys Satan with death. In order to destroy all of the dark matter, he must also then let our physical bodies die, so all dark matter can be destroyed.

If God or the "universal brain" knows I have a soul, he will not care as much about the well-being of my physical body, especially if he has already saved my spiritual one. He does care about my body, but he knows I won't truly succumb to death if my soul is saved. If I do not save my soul before my physical body dies, then death wins. If my soul is saved, God can destroy both my physical body and death. In that case, God and I both win! That's how God defeats death with death!

> *The righteous perish, and no one takes it to heart; the devout are taken away, and no one understands that the righteous are taken away to be spared from evil. Those who walk uprightly enter into peace; they find rest as they lie in death. (Isaiah 57: 1–2, New International Version)*

Matter creates life; dark matter breaks down life, and antimatter destroys all physical matter, leaving only "spiritual" antimatter in the universe. Our physical/biological universe comes to an end, leaving the other spiritual universe. If my body and soul are separate, I can live for eternity in that spiritual universe, because when our physical/biological universe ends, ***time ends with it! Remember, even Einstein says time can be manipulated!***

If our physical/biological universe consists of life and death, and physical matter is life, why can't dark matter be death? If there were dark matter particles inside our own atoms, "spiritual" antimatter would need to destroy all matter in order to completely destroy death. That's why God gave us souls, so he could destroy all matter and still save us. I believe our souls are made with "spiritual" antimatter, and that's why our souls can live!

So in that line of thinking, couldn't God, our "universal brain" create a being that had a soul that had so much "spiritual" antimatter generating from it that dark matter could not penetrate his body? Could that be what made Jesus (the Son of God) physically? Perhaps the "spiritual" antimatter and his own brain had a constant open connection to the "universal brain" or God. That's why his sacrifice was so special. He had a body that dark matter could not penetrate; death could not touch him, and he was not supposed to die. Jesus died and gave part of his body to us, so that we could not die, and that created the sacrifice! That's why they say he was the pure lamb, and now he comes back as the lion to destroy all matter—both physical and dark matter. He will end the battle of good and evil.

> *Since therefore the children share in flesh and blood, he himself likewise partook of the same things, that through death he might destroy the one who has the power of death, that is, the devil. (Hebrews 2:14, English Standard Version)*

I think that's also why the resurrection was so special; Jesus was sacrificed and put to death, and death was allowed to take him. God did not forget or forsake Jesus. Jesus gave the ultimate sacrifice of a pure body with faith God would save him. Once Jesus gave his pure body to death on faith, God saved and resurrected him. God did not forget his child! After Jesus sacrificed his body so we could have a part of his pure body inside of us, we were all saved. This allowed God to destroy death without destroying us in the process! Jesus had a body and soul with so much "spiritual" antimatter that dark matter could not penetrate it. I believe this is why Jesus's physical body was raised to heaven.

The Bible says God is alive inside us. This supports the idea that our brains could be connected to a "universal brain," and this principle also applies to our souls. Our bodies give off energy. Is it possible for us to generate "spiritual" antimatter on a quantum level by making certain particles vibrate at a special frequency? Could "spiritual" antimatter (a soul) be created if you took a male chromosome particle and a female chromosome and made their quarks vibrate in perfect harmony?

If we could create "spiritual" antimatter with our own bodies, we could destroy all the physical matter in the universe, and eventually we would be saved and destroy death in the process. Life and all physical matter would also be destroyed, leaving only the spiritual universe. I think that by believing and praying, our bodies could generate "spiritual" antimatter. That's why Jesus tells us to pray: because we create "spiritual" antimatter and we connect with that "universal brain" or God. Could praying just makes all the quarks in your body vibrate at the perfect frequency to connect with the universe?

If we could create "spiritual" antimatter, then we could probably also create dark matter or dark energy. It seems possible that our particles, on a quantum level, are capable of giving off dark energy, and this depends on our attitudes and beliefs; because we are making them vibrate at different frequencies.

If you want to change your life and the energy around you, start praying and believing in God, our "universal brain," and try to create that "spiritual" antimatter and energy around you. Maybe that's why our world is so crazy right now. It's full of too many bad attitudes giving of too much dark energy! We are creating this dark energy as a by-product of our attitudes and actions. It sure makes you think about karma; what goes around comes around! But based on my theory, all you have to do is change your attitude and change your actions; then the spiritual energy around you will change. You just need to believe it exists in the first place!

Now that you have gotten this far into my theory, take a moment to remember the beginning. Think about everything we have covered and all the possible connections! Does it make you question how you look at your own universe and life in general? It made me change my view on life and the universe, and I like to think at least a couple of these dots are interesting connections.

MOTHER EARTH OR MOTHER UNIVERSE

I consider this section the last part of my theory and how I finish viewing everything.

People have always referred to our earth as "Mother Nature" or "Mother Earth." Why? We live on earth, and it's the only place in the universe we have found life. That's why I believe the universe itself is alive; we are just part of the bigger organism, like the baby in the mother's womb.

If we take God, our "universal brain" and add him into the mix, we get our Heavenly Father or (HF). It's finally time to explain those symbols I told you to remember. I also mentioned a Physical Child or (PC) in the previous section; we are also going to add that into this equation.

I called it an equation because this is what we are going to end up with by the end of my thought. This is my attempt at what I think a formula for life should resemble. For you for all you scientists, I have never taken physics in my life, so you will have to let me know how I do on my first attempt. This is also my attempt to also add some biology and spiritual factors into this equation, since I have been saying we need to include other elements in our hunt for answers to the universe.

Before I begin, I just want to ask this question: why does an equation that explains everything overall have to be complicated? Mine is very simple. We often assume that the answers to important questions will always result in some outrageous mathematical problem only one or two people may ever figure out. Why can't life be simple? I don't believe that my formula is an equation for everything, but could it work to explain mankind?

Here we go, let's see how well I explain this. I first looked at our universe and took the three parts I thought were important: the physical part, the biological part, and the spiritual aspect. Then I came up with this equation based on my theory. If we are going to come up with an equation for life, we need it to reflect how life works. It should consist of two opposite halves that make a whole being, just like the sperm and egg. Let's make it even simpler: we need a mother and a father.

This is where I am going to use our symbols. We have our father, our Heavenly Father or Father Time (HF). There is also a mother, Mother Universe (MU). Now that we have our two universal opposites, let's examine their dimensions. God or the "universal brain" dwells in the parallel universe and is zero-dimensional, so we are going to add that factor in and make our (HF) into $(HF)^{0 \mid \infty}$. The zero indicates he is a zero-dimensional entity. The infinity symbol represents his omnipresence, both in our physical universe and our parallel "spiritual" universe.

Next let's take our Mother Universe (MU) and add its dimensional level symbol. Since our physical universe consists of all the dimensions we could visit in our universe, MU also gets the infinity symbol. She is multidimensional and everywhere, but since she has dimensions, she does not get a zero: only the infinity symbol. $(MU)^{\infty}$.

Since we really want to know why we are here, we want the answer from our equation to represent us as humankind. We are all after that one answer: how we got here and why we are here.

$$(HF)^{0 \;\; \infty} + (MU)^{\infty} = ?$$

I want to note that another reason I used the infinity sign is to reflect the never-ending expansion of the universe.

This is my representation of the universe. It has the physical aspect of trying to figure out why we are here as humans by including our "physical mother" or physical universe, it also has the biological aspect of trying to figure out why we are here, because it includes a mother/father factor. It also includes a spiritual aspect by including a spiritual father, the opposite of a physical mother, thus reflecting nature's opposites. I also included the dimension factor in the equation. Why can't a simple equation like this answer all of our questions?

Since we are combing a father and mother in this equation, I would assume the result would be a child. That's where our Physical Child (PH) symbol will come back into play. I believe this would be the answer to my equation: a Physical Child with a soul or spirit.

Mother Earth or Mother Universe

$$(HF)^{0 \cdot \infty} + (MU)^{\infty} = (PC)^{0 \mid \infty}$$

The (HF) represents "spiritual" antimatter in my theory; the (MU) represents all physical matter and dark matter as well. When combined, we get a Physical Child (PC), and that represents humankind in the universe. The zero and the infinity signs represent two different factors, so they can't really be added together. One represents our spiritual side from our (HF), specifically our soul within our physical bodies. The infinity sign represents all the dimension levels the soul can travel in our physical universe through a possible out-of-body experience. Our physical universe is expanding and infinite, so we have the infinity sign. This is also why I believe our souls are meant to travel the universe, not our physical bodies. I think the stars are just hints at what is possible. Our physical bodies are not meant to travel in space. I think we were physically meant to stay on solid ground.

LIFE AND DEATH

As humans, why don't we study life and death with more depth? We study the universe scientifically and physically. We study modern medicine to understand how our bodies work physically and biologically. Religion studies death but does so from a theological perspective rather than a scientific or biologic perspective. Life and death are the two greatest mysteries of humankind, yet we don't seem to study it. We simply go about our days hoping we don't die!

Life and death are the two greatest experiences of our life; we can experience them only once. While many of us believe we have souls that will live on after our deaths, we are still afraid. Why do we look at the stars for the answers to life when they are just rocks?

If we studied life and death more, we might discover more answers. When we do study life, though, we only study how it works and how to prevent death. We don't study why life works, and we barely study death or what really happens when we die. If you believe in God, you should not fear death but try to understand it so you can live this life to the fullest. I think one of the reasons we don't study death is because it reminds us of people who have passed away. But if you believe in God or the "universal brain," wouldn't you want to understand death to find those people? Those people are only gone if you believe they are gone. If you believe in God or the "universal brain," then the souls of our departed must be out there somewhere.

We look to the stars because we still feel a spiritual and biological connection with God, our "universal brain." Science believes that space is a place for physical bodies, but I believe it is a place for spiritual bodies. These spiritual bodies may travel there after death or through out-of-body experiences. What better way to show your faith to God than to stare death in the face and not fear it? Learn from it so we can understand it; then destroy it!

Would physicists find "spiritual" antimatter (a soul or spirit) leave the body when someone passed away if we studied people at the point of death?

The meaning of life is to find a way to conquer death. Thankfully, religion tells me how to do that correctly!

When we study life, we know that the miracle happens when those two special cells come together and form one new being. Why don't we study that miracle more? Quantum physics works at that molecular level and is trying to send particles to a different dimension. While starting life, when we are at that cell or molecular level, our soul would be coming into this universe from a parallel spiritual one (through the white hole), why don't we study life and its creation at a quantum level?

Why doesn't science work with modern medicine to better understand that miracle? Sperm and egg start the miracle of life; why don't quantum physicists work with those particles? Life starts small. I think we need to start that search on the quantum level, with particles from biological brain cells or reproductive cells. As I mentioned before, I believe if we studied life, we would find a white hole with a soul coming through that dimension portal. *I believe souls could be "spiritual" antimatter!*

The question of why we are here is such a universal question that it is going to take the universe (everyone) to figure it out. Here is an article I found online suggesting science might have found evidence of souls.

Does the soul exist? Evidence says "yes"!

The reality of the soul is among the most important questions of life. Although religions go on and on about its existence, how do we know if souls really exist? A string of new scientific experiments helps answer this ancient spiritual question.

The idea of the soul is bound up with the idea of a future life and our belief in a continued existence after death. It's said to be the ultimate animating principle by which we think and feel, but isn't dependent on the body. Many infer its existence without scientific analysis or reflection. Indeed, the mysteries of birth and death, the play of consciousness during dreams (or after a few martinis), and even the commonest <u>mental</u> operations – such as imagination and memory – suggest the existence of a vital life force – an *élan vital* – that exists independent of the body.

Yet, the current scientific paradigm doesn't recognize this spiritual dimension of life. We're told we're just the activity of carbon and some proteins; we live awhile and die; and the universe? It too has no meaning. It has all been worked out in the equations – no need for a soul. But biocentrism – a new 'theory of everything' – challenges this traditional, materialistic model of reality. In all <u>directions</u>, this outdated paradigm leads to insoluble enigmas, to ideas that are ultimately irrational. But knowledge is the prelude to wisdom, and soon our worldview will catch up with the facts.

Of course, most spiritual people view the soul as emphatically more definitive than the scientific concept. It's considered the incorporeal essence of a person, and is said to be immortal and transcendent of material existence. But when scientists speak of the soul (if at all), it's usually in a materialistic context, or treated as a poetic synonym for the mind. Everything knowable about the "soul" can be learned by studying the functioning of the brain. In their view, neuroscience is the only branch of scientific study relevant to understanding the soul.

Traditionally, science has dismissed the soul as an object of human belief, or reduced it to a psychological concept that shapes our cognition of the observable natural world. The terms "life" and "death" are thus nothing more than the common concepts of "biological life" and "biological death." The animating principle is simply the laws of chemistry and physics. You (and all the poets and philosophers that ever lived) are just dust orbiting the core of the Milky Way galaxy.

As I sit here in my office surrounded by piles of scientific books, I can't find a single reference to the soul, or any notion of an immaterial, eternal essence that occupies our being. Indeed, a soul has never been seen under an electron microscope, nor spun in the laboratory in a test tube or ultra-centrifuge. According to these books, nothing appears to survive the human body after death.

While neuroscience has made tremendous progress illuminating the functioning of the brain, why we have a subjective experience remains mysterious. The problem of the soul lies exactly here, in understanding the nature of the self, the "I" in existence that feels and lives life. But this isn't just a problem for biology and cognitive science, but for the whole of Western natural philosophy itself.

Our current worldview – the world of objectivity and naïve realism – is beginning to show fatal cracks. Of course, this will not surprise many of the philosophers and other readers who, contemplating the works of men such as Plato, Socrates and Kant, and of Buddha and other great spiritual teachers, kept wondering about the relationship between the universe and the mind of man.

Recently, biocentrism and other scientific theories have also started to challenge the old physico-chemical paradigm, and to ask some of the difficult questions about life: Is there a soul? Does anything endure the ravages of time?

Life and consciousness are central to this new view of being, reality and the cosmos. Although the current scientific paradigm is based on the belief that the world has an objective observer-independent existence, real experiments suggest just the opposite. We think life is just the activity of atoms and particles, which spin around for a while and then dissipate into nothingness. But if we add life to the equation, we can explain some of the major puzzles of modern science, including the uncertainty principle, entanglement, and the fine-tuning of the laws that shape the universe.

Consider the famous two-slit experiment. When you watch a particle go through the holes, it behaves like a bullet, passing through one slit or the other. But if no one observes the particle, it exhibits the behavior of a wave and can pass through both slits at the same time. This and other experiments tell us that unobserved particles exist only as 'waves of probability' as the great Nobel laureate Max Born demonstrated in 1926. They're statistical predictions – nothing but a likely outcome. Until observed, they have no real existence; only when the mind sets the scaffolding in place, can they be thought of as having duration or a position in space. Experiments make it increasingly clear that even *mere knowledge in the experimenter's mind* is sufficient to convert possibility to reality.

Many scientists dismiss the implications of these experiments, because until recently, this observer-dependent behavior was thought to be confined to the subatomic world. However, this is being challenged by researchers around the world. In fact, just this year a team of physicists (Gerlich et al, **Nature Communications** 2:263, 2011) showed that quantum weirdness also occurs in the human-scale world. They studied huge compounds composed of up to 430 atoms, and confirmed that this strange quantum behavior extends into the larger world we live in.

Importantly, this has a direct bearing on the question of whether humans and other living creatures have souls. As Kant pointed out over 200 years ago, everything we experience – including all the colors, sensations and objects we perceive – are nothing but representations in our mind. Space and time are simply the mind's tools for putting it all together. Now, to the amusement of idealists, scientists are beginning dimly to recognize that those rules make existence itself possible. Indeed, the experiments above suggest that objects only exist with real properties if they are observed. The results not only defy our classical intuition, but suggest that a part of the mind – the soul – is immortal and exists outside of space and time.

"The hope of another life" wrote Will Durant "gives us courage to meet our own death, and to bear with the death of our loved ones; we are twice armed if we fight with faith." And we are thrice armed if we fight with science.

"Psychology Today" Published on December 21, 2011 by Robert Lanza, M.D. in Biocentrism
http://www.psychologytoday.com/blog/biocentrism/201112/does-the-soul-exist-evidence-says-yes

Here is another article by two other quantum physicists suggesting the soul enters the universe upon death.

Near-death experiences occur when the soul leaves the nervous system and enters the universe, claim two quantum physics experts.

A near-death experience happens when quantum substances which form the soul leave the nervous system and enter the universe at large, according to a remarkable theory proposed by two eminent scientists.

According to this idea, consciousness is a program for a quantum computer in the brain which can persist in the universe even after death, explaining the perceptions of those who have near-death experiences.

Dr. Stuart Hameroff, Professor Emeritus at the Departments of Anesthesiology and Psychology and the Director of the Centre of Consciousness Studies at the University of Arizona, has advanced the quasi-religious theory.

It is based on a quantum theory of consciousness he and British physicist Sir Roger Penrose have developed which holds that the essence of our soul is contained inside structures called microtubules within brain cells.

They have argued that our experience of consciousness is the result of quantum gravity effects in these microtubules, a theory which they dubbed orchestrated objective reduction (Orch-OR).

Thus it is held that our souls are more than the interaction of neurons in the brain. They are in fact constructed from the very fabric of the universe - and may have existed since the beginning of time.

"Mail Online" published by Damian Gayle October 30, 2012
http://www.dailymail.co.uk/sciencetech/article-2225190/Can-quantum-physics-explain-bizarre-experiences-patients-brought-brink-death.html

HOW SCIENCE AND RELIGION COMPARE

Science and religion have always engaged in a head-to-head battle. If you can't tell by now, this book is not about the battle but about connecting the dots.

As science and religion have debated, we have found many similarities. The Bible did make these claims well before science could prove them. I am not going to list all the similarities I found while researching, but I will name a few important ones. In my theory, time is not a factor for a spiritual entity, so you need to remember that when reading these examples.

The Bible refers to the creation of the universe in the chapter of Genesis. When reading these verses, consider it without time.

> ***In the beginning God created the heavens and the earth. (Genesis 1:1, New International Version)***

God has no time constraint, so scientifically this could include the moment of the big bang all the way through the creation of our physical universe, solar system, and earth. When people think of this statement, they imagine the world already evolved and filled with life. I imagine it simpler than that. I think of it still down at a molecular level. God knew the ingredients were there, and he set the plan in motion. He knew what the universe would eventually become, even when our solar system was still just ingredients in the mixing bowl.

> ***Now the earth was formless and empty, darkness was over the surface of the deep, and the Spirit of God was hovering over the waters. (Genesis 1:2, New International Version)***

The solar system was still evolving and the earth was taking shape but was not fully formed. This verse indicates the sun was probably not formed yet either. If the sun was not formed fully, it probably was not yet producing enough energy to emit light strong enough to reach the earth.

> *Then God said, "Let there be light," and there was light, and God saw that light was good. Then he separated the light from the darkness. God called the light "day" and the darkness "night" and evening passed and morning came, marking the first day. (Genesis 1:3–5, New International Version)*

The earth and solar system had finished forming, and the sun had started producing enough energy to reach earth, creating the first day and night, since time is still physically in motion and our universe is evolving and growing. Just like a physical/biological being growing from birth, our universe is alive. When those first beams of sunlight hit earth, it created the first day and night.

This sure sounds like the big bang, evolution, and the creation of our universe; especially if time does not exist to an entity like God, our "universal brain." If the first three verses of the Bible can fit, then this could make for a long book. But you can see how everything fits if time can be manipulated physically (proved by Einstein). Why would we ever even consider time to be a factor for an entity like God?

Here are just a few more similarities for you from the Bible.

> *There is one glory of the sun, another glory of the moon, and another glory of the stars; for star differs from star in glory. (Corinthians 15:41, New American Standard Version)*

As we observe stars with the naked eye, they can look similar, like points of light and energy. Reports from science have shown us that the analysis of their light spectra reveals that each star is unique and differs from all others. How could someone from the first century have known something like that? The Bible describes the earth suspended in space. Today we know that the earth literally floats in space.

How Science and Religion Compare

He stretches out the north over empty space; he hangs the earth on nothing. (Job 26:7, New American Standard Version)

We could go on comparing the Bible and science. My point is that, without the time factor, the Bible seems very consistent with everything we now know scientifically about the universe.

THE ALPHA AND THE OMEGA

Alpha and Omega is the first and last letters in the Greek alphabet; they are also an appellation of God or Jesus Christ in the book of Revelation.

> *I am the Alpha and the Omega, the first and the last, the beginning and the end. (Revelations 22:13, New International Version)*

If our universe is biological and alive, it will, like us, eventually die before it also returns to its creator. This also means that we could kill our universe and earth if we are not careful; we may destroy the secrets to the universe if they are here before we ever even find them. We need to take much better care of our whole universe if it is alive and we are part of it. God does tell us of the end of days, or the end of time—the end of our physical/biological universe. It sounds like the Bible's book of Revelation is a scientific possibility. The only way to escape the destruction of this physical universe is to be saved in the spiritual universe!

That is the meaning of life to me: escape death, and find God before time runs out! Learn to live forever in the spiritual realm. God is life. To live eternally is to find God.

Alpha and Omega are opposites and refer to time: the beginning and the end. If a "universal brain" exists and created the physical universe, he will also be there when it dies.

CONCLUSION
What I Think Einstein Was Truly After

You have now read my entire theory and how I try to make sense of the universe around me. I want to try to open up people's minds and try to make them think "what if." I want to remind them that anything is possible, even God. If our universe is truly alive, I think we need to not only study more than the planets and stars. We need to study life and death as well, because I think that there are many unanswered questions that lie there. We also need to embrace God as a society if we ever want to figure out his miracles. After all, you need to study a magician to understand his tricks.

If the answers to the universe were just floating around in space in these dense masses of different matter, don't you think we would have found something, anything, by now? Maybe we did find it already and just didn't look at it from the right angle? The only things we have actually found in space are hints, clues to the big puzzle of the universe. The only place we've found life is here on Earth, so maybe we should start looking here to answer life's questions. If we looked at matter, dark matter, and "spiritual" antimatter together, we might unlock some answers about the role of "spiritual" antimatter in the universe.

We all know Einstein was ultimately after an equation that would simply explain the universe. I think he was really trying to find and prove the existence of God. He was asking the same question I am asking: why are we here, and how do we fit into this universe? I think Einstein was particularly interested in these questions because of the outbreak of World War II. He was a German who didn't approve of what the Nazis were doing, and people said that as a child Einstein had believed in God. He didn't lose his faith as he grew up; he was hiding it from Nazi Germany. I believe he was smart enough to know when to keep his mouth shut.

Since World War II was on the verge of breaking out, Einstein knew people had the potential to start a war that was going to kill millions and possibly destroy the world. I think he was trying to prove there was a God in order to stop that war and prevent it from erupting. I think that he thought that if he could find that universal equation and prove to mankind there was a God, he could stop World War II and save humanity. That's why I personally think that until we bring that God factor into the equation, we will never truly finish his work. We need to think like Einstein, and I think he believed in God. That's why I think we will never finish or figure out a universal equation until we introduce the God factor. That's what I believe! God bless and amen. Don't forget:

Religion tells us what God did; science explains how he did it.
—Unknown

As the body without the spirit is dead, so faith without deeds is dead!
(James 2:26, New International Version)

That's my theory. What's yours? Come visit my web page.
www.Facebook.com/ItsAllRelativeTheGodFactor

The End

www.ingramcontent.com/pod-product-compliance
Lightning Source LLC
Chambersburg PA
CBHW040457240426
43665CB00038B/14